Heavy Horses of the World

Heavy Horses of the World

Valerie Russell

Heart Prairie Press

Frontispiece: *Norikers in their sometimes lush, sometimes harsh homeland* – Austria.

Copyright © 1983 Valerie Russell. All rights reserved. No part of this publication may be reproduced, stored in a retrieval system or transmitted, in any form or by any means, electronic, mechanical, photocopying, recording or otherwise, without the permission of the publisher and the copyright owner.

Published in 1992 by:
Heart Prairie Press
P. O. Box 332
Whitewater, Wisconsin, 53190 USA
ISBN 0-9622663-8-8
by arrangement with Chancellor Press
part of Reed International Books

First published in 1983 by
Country Life Books, England.
ISBN 0 600 36831 9

Pubisher's Cataloging in Publication

Russell, Valerie.
    Heavy horses of the world / Valerie Russell. —2nd edition.
    p.: ill. cm.
    Includes bibliographical references and index.
    ISBN 0-9622663-8-8

    1. Draft horses—History. I. Title.
SF3 11.R8   636.1'5
                        QBI91-1611

Produced by Mandarin Offset
Printed in Hong Kong

Contents

Preface	7
Heavy Horses – Past, Present, and Future	9
The Ardennes	12
The Australian Draught	19
The Belgian Heavy Draught	25
The Boulonnais	33
The Breton	36
The Clydesdale	40
The Dutch Heavy Draught	50

The Hungarian Breeds
    The Hungarian Heavy Draught
    The Murakozi
	52

The Italian Draught or Agricultural Heavy Horse	56
The Jutland	57
The Noriker	62
The North Swedish	66
The Percheron	70
The Rhenish-German Heavy	80

The Russian Heavy Breeds
    The Lithuanian Heavy Harness Horse
    The Russian Heavy Draught
    The Soviet Heavy Draught
    The Vladimir Heavy Draught
	82

The Schleswig-Holstein Heavy	90
The Shire	94
The Suffolk	106
Heavy-Horse Harness	114
Horses in Competition	118
Bibliography	126
Acknowledgements	126
Index	127

Preface

The initial planning of a book and the form it finally takes can be two rather different things, particularly when some of the topics included are breaking new ground. The original planning of this book involved, first of all, selecting *which* of the heavy horse breeds around the world to include. The temptation to include everything that could – even remotely – be called 'heavy' was enormous, but had to be resisted. A fairly arbitrary means of selection was used – resulting in the rejection of almost everything whose size and proportions did not quite fit in with the popular image of 'the gentle giant'.

It was also envisaged that such well-known breeds as the Shire, Percheron, Belgian, and so on, would merit longer than average chapters, and the less well-known would merit shorter chapters of almost equal length. In the event, the Breed Societies of, for example, the Australian Draught Horse and the Danish Jutland, provided such a wealth of interesting information that much of what they sent just *had* to be included.

This was balanced by the less helpful Breed Societies – including the one which responded to my letter of enquiry thus: 'If we answered all your questions we could write the book ourselves, and we do not have time for that.' (Luckily, information on that breed was forthcoming from other sources.)

For some other breeds, the type of information which I required was just not forthcoming, yet the breed had to be included because of its past status, or for the sake of completeness.

Although the information I sought from each Breed Society was basically the same, what I *received* (or what was available) varied according to whether the breed was being used on a strictly commercial basis (as in most continental European countries), or largely for publicity purposes, or as a hobby (as in Britain, North America, and Australia). The former tended to be specific, with emphasis on height, weight and performance; the latter more anecdotal.

An interesting point was that of all the breeders, the Hungarians and the Russians were the only ones who dispassionately pointed out the conformational faults of their animals. Little is known about the heavy horses of these countries outside their own borders, and it was especially gratifying to receive material from them.

Possibly the most limiting factor in research of this kind is language. A significant amount of material was received in foreign languages. To have it translated would appear, at first sight, to be perfectly simple. This was by no means so. As anyone who is involved, even slightly, with the horse world knows, it has a language all of its own. To be sure of extracting the real meaning from a foreign text, the translator must be familiar not only with the language of the country concerned, but also with the technical terms of the horse world. I can only hope that as a result, no serious misinterpretations appear in the text.

There are, inevitably, errors of omission in a book of this kind, and for whatever reason, there may be errors of fact, even though great care has been taken to avoid the latter. If any reader has any further information about heavy horses in any part of the world, I would be most grateful to receive it, with a view to inclusion in any future editions.

Opposite *A pair of Shires ploughing. The horses' ability to work land without compacting it allows better drainage in many soils.*

Below *An unusual harness turn-out of Percherons at Haras du Pin.*

Heavy Horses – Past, Present, and Future

Fifteen or twenty years ago, heavy-horse breeders in Britain, and in many other countries around the world, could talk with enthusiasm about the past glories of their particular breed. They spoke with less certainty about the present. When it came to the future, a silence would fall. Few of those involved in the heavy horse world at that time could see very much future for their beloved 'heavies'.

Today, the picture has changed almost completely. Less time is spent on reminiscing about the 'old days'; the present is full of activity; the future, in most cases, appears full of promise.

In the following pages the history of the individual breeds of heavy horse, their rise to pre-eminence in the rural economy of their respective countries, and their decline, will be told. All heavy horses, however, have a number of things in common – or nearly so. To avoid tedious repetition, therefore, a brief outline of their history as a genus may not come amiss.

It is generally thought that the heavy horses of the present day are descended from one of the two basic groups of equines that survived the last Ice Age. This group, known as the Northern or Coldblood horse, developed in what is now northern Europe, in lands of adequate rainfall which encouraged lush pasture and thick forest.

Abundance of grazing meant that the indigenous horses did not need to move far for food; thus they developed into the bulky, slow-moving Forest or Diluvial horse from which the modern heavy breeds are descended. In more recent times, the descendants of these were found in large numbers in what are now the Low Countries, and particularly in Flanders. As will be recounted, these Flanders or Flemish horses play an important part in the immediate ancestry of many European breeds such as the Shire, the Clydesdale, the Belgian and others.

The following chapters will tell, too, of how heavy horses were used as pack animals, farm horses, war horses and dray horses; how they declined in many countries, and how they are now making a welcome recovery.

One of the principal reasons for the present increase in the use of 'heavies' (modest though it is, so far) is the dramatic increase in the price of fossil fuel. A number of tasks that were previously done by lorry, truck or tractor, are now actually done more cheaply by horse. Some examples are given in the following pages. As the price of fuel seems likely to go on increasing, it also seems likely that horses could be used in more and more situations – although the days of the great horse teams of Canada, Australia and the United States must surely be a thing of the past, barring some totally unforeseen catastrophe. But

Opposite A familiar scene in pre-Second-World-War Britain – going home from the fields.

Right Past, present, and possibly future. The tractor replaced the heavy horse in the immediate past. Is the heavy horse about to make a significant comeback?

Above   *An old engraving of the Flemish Horse – the horse from which many of the European heavy breeds are derived, and a descendant of the pre-historic Forest or Diluvial horse.*

Opposite   *A pair of Shires engaged in logging activities.*

on small farms, in even so highly a mechanised country as Canada, heavy horses are once more being used, and in some instances are the *sole* source of draught power. They are also being used increasingly in forestry in many countries, as they do less damage and can work on land too steep for tractors.

The heavy-horse enthusiasts are watching with interest and satisfaction, and are emphasising the advantages of horse as opposed to tractor power. While these advantages need to be kept in perspective, it is interesting to mention some of them. Horses have, of course, always had some advantages over tractors: they do not depreciate so quickly, and they provide their own replacements – at far less cost. To a large extent, too, they pay for the cost of their own food, and they help fertilise the ground in which that food is grown. So much is reasonably obvious.

What perhaps is less obvious to the casual observer (though not to the farmer) is that land worked by horses is, in many instances, *better* than that worked by tractors. For instance, tractors are notorious for the compaction they cause, particularly on certain soils. Horses do not compact soil, and it has been suggested that, even on farms that are highly mechanised, horses could be employed profitably in cultivating field headlands badly damaged by tractors as they turn. In addition, horses can often work land earlier in the season, when it is still unfit for tractors.

The general state of the soil is giving cause for concern in some highly mechanised farming countries, such as Britain, which use large quantities of chemical fertilisers and sprays, and so on. The combination of heavy machinery causing compaction and fertilisers which destroy soil micro-organisms is altering the soil structure, and not for the better.

The difference between horse- and tractor-grown crops is described by Roger Clark, well-known breeder of Suffolk horses, who uses them for farming. He was comparing a stretch of land prepared by horse and sown with corn, with a piece by its side ploughed by tractor:

…and when the corn was about six inches high and you looked at it from the road, the bit that was ploughed with horses was far greener and denser and taller, and looked a lot better than the piece that had been done by tractor. You could see where the horses finished and the tractor started. It was not only my observation but also the farm foreman – a rare mechanised man, and a good chap too…

Those are the more serious disadvantages of high mechanisation but, on a lighter note, there are other things horses can be trained to do that tractors (unless they become remote-controlled) cannot manage. Horses can be trained to work by word of mouth and without reins. For example, one farmer trained his horse to work without him when drilling for seed. The man was up on a wagon opening bags of seed, and when he wanted to fill the drill, he called his horse to come towards him, turn, and back the drill up to the wagon so he could fill it. He then set the horse off down the field again – all without climbing off the wagon. A tractor will not do that!

But, let us be quite clear, a wholesale return to horse power is unlikely to happen – yet the future of the heavy horse now seems assured. In the following chapters their increased use and popularity are made plain, and let us hope that never again do the conditions of the twenty years preceding the 1960s recur. The heavy horse is back from the brink. May he never approach it again.

The Ardennes

The setting is a showground at Vittel in northern France, the occasion the annual show of the French Ardennes Heavy Horse Breeders' Society. The show is reaching its spectacular climax. At the far end of the arena twenty-two Ardennes horses – mares, stallions and geldings, averaging three-quarters of a ton each, and harnessed together in line abreast – start advancing at an active yet weighty trot, encouraged by white-clad men cracking whips. The horses forge relentlessly and powerfully onward, approaching nearer and nearer to the judges at the top of the arena until on a word of command they stop – as if they were one animal – and stand motionless, a solid wall of controlled equine strength.

In those few tense minutes are encapsulated the qualities of power and willingness, of calmness and obedience that have earned these great animals (and other heavy horses round the world) their affectionately bestowed title of 'the gentle giants'.

The Ardennes horse has evolved in those hilly, wooded regions on either side of the Franco-Belgian border from which the breed takes its name. It is an ancient breed, mentioned in the writings of Julius Caesar and Herodotus, and has, in common with its near relative, the Belgian Heavy Draught, been less influenced by outside blood than many other breeds.

There is evidence of the existence of a race of horses (smaller than today's breed) in the region since pre-historic times, and it is suggested that the Ardennes are the direct descendants of horses, 50,000 years old, of which remains were found at Solutre in the Saone-sur-Loire. While discussion about their precise origins continues, there is no doubt that the ancestors of the present horses played their part in the history of both France and Belgium. Julius Caesar, visiting the region when it was known as Gaul, praised the native horses for their stamina and hardiness, and the French marshal, Vicomte Turenne, in the 12th

Above Coquette du Bourneau and her one-day-old foal on a British farm. A small number of Ardennes have been imported into Britain and some are being used in agriculture.

Opposite Ardennes mare and foal during the Ardennes National Championships at Vittel, France in 1981.

Above The impressive sight of a line of Ardennes horses advancing down the show ground during the annual show at Vittel in France.

Opposite Ardennes horses are still used in French vineyards. This scene is at Beaucaire in Provence.

century, was impressed by them and used them as mounts for his troops. In the periods of peace during the Middle Ages, the size of the breed was increased to meet the demands of agriculture – work for which these horses are supremely suitable and in which they have been employed right up to and including the present time. But this more peaceful pursuit has inevitably been interrupted by wars. Napoleon is believed to have used Ardennes horses for hauling heavy artillery in the disastrous Russian campaign of 1812, and in the First World War they were used extensively for moving vehicles and guns, and particularly for pulling them out of the appalling morasses of the Flanders mud.

Originally the French and Belgian Ardennes were a single breed, but as national borders became more firmly established they went their separate ways to some extent, although the only noticeable result has been an increase in size of the Belgian Ardennes. However, because of the relative isolation of their mountainous homeland, neither was subject to much outside blood in their early history, except for some oriental blood in the Middle Ages, and both have remained much more pure than some other breeds. Nevertheless it seems appropriate to discuss the two types separately, as each has its own breed society and its own stud book.

The French Ardennes is bred in almost all of north-eastern France, from the east of the Parisian basin to the Rhône, from the spur of the Juras and the Massif Central to the German and French borders (where breeding is chiefly in the hands of studs at Montier-en-Der and Rosières-aux-Salines). Breeding also occurs widely outside the original Ardennes area, particularly in the south-east of France. There are, altogether nearly 300 stallions and about 5,000 mares registered in the entire country.

During the 19th century, some Belgian Heavy Draught blood was introduced in certain areas with the aim of obtaining bigger-boned, stockier, stronger horses, better suited to the heavy ground in the east of France. The size certainly did increase in those areas, but the imports were not, apparently, always of very good quality, and are held accountable for the deterioration of the limbs that plagued the breed, especially in the early part of the 20th century.

Over the years, three types have developed, due largely to the demands of the different regions and to the soil and climate. The 'classic' Ardennes is found in the eastern regions – Champagne, Lorraine, Alsace and Franche-Comte – and is the smallest and possibly the nearest to the original horse. The Auxois Ardennes, found in the Cluny area, is stocky, very powerful, and a larger version of the classic, while in the north (in small numbers) is the Northern Ardennes, formerly known as the Trait du Nord, which is the largest of all. For most practical purposes the breed is regarded as having two types – the classic and the Auxois – with the stallions of the former standing between 15 hands and 15.2 hands (152.4 and 157.5 cm) and the latter from 15.2 to 16 hands (157.5 to 162.6 cm). Horses standing more than 16.3 hands (170.2 cm) are not liked.

In appearance the Ardennes is a very close-coupled, chunky horse, with short, strong legs, a very thick, muscular neck, and massive shoulders – a picture of compact strength. It has a small, expressive head, with a straight or even slightly dished profile, and a squareness of the muzzle that is said to indicate its ancient origins. The eyes are bright and intelligent, contained in prominent sockets, and the ears small and pointed. The neck, crested in the case of stallions, is exceptionally thick and muscular; although this is an indication of great strength and draught power, it can present practical problems – at least to Ardennes owners in Britain. It is extremely difficult to find a collar to fit.

The Ardennes body is very solid indeed, with a rounded, well-sprung rib cage; the chest is deep and wide, the loins strong, the back short and muscular, the haunches wide, and the hindquarters long and heavily muscled. The shoulders are well-sloped. The legs, as well as being short, have enormous bone and wide, strong joints. They have a moderate amount of feather, and although they do not show quite the 'tree-trunk' appearance of, for example, the Belgian and Dutch Draughts, they are nonetheless substantial. The Ardennes have exceptionally good feet, with hard blue horn, and because of centuries of pounding the paved roads of France they have, by a process of the survival of the fittest, become very tough indeed, and do not need shoeing when working on anything but the roughest land.

There is a considerable range of colours in the Ardennes. The most common are the pink bay and the strawberry roan, usually with 'badger-coloured' mane and tail, but there are also blue roans (with grey-black manes and tail), dark or liver chestnut, bay-brown, and a very light colour, almost Palomino, with blond mane and tail, which looks absolutely superb. Most have black feathering, giving them the appearance of wearing black boots. Blacks and greys are not admitted by the breed society.

An interesting and unusual colour change occurs in some Ardennes when they lose their winter coats. In common with other breeds, they grow a long winter coat, 2 or 3 in. (5 or 7.6 cm.) in length, under which is a finer, shorter one. In the spring, the long winter coat is shed, revealing a short coat that has become almost white – and this gradually changes to the normal colour for the remainder of the summer.

In France the Ardennes are still used to some extent for agricultural purposes, particularly on hill farms and, more widely, for removing 'clearings' in forestry undertakings. They are not used very much in harness these days, although a few are still employed in the vineyards of Alsace. Most horses start work at the age of about three years.

The first French Ardennes were imported into Britain in 1975, and there are now about twenty of the breed in the country – all of the smaller type. They are used for a variety of agricultural work. Their hardiness and ability to live out and thrive on comparatively poor fare (a characteristic resulting from the harshness of their native environment) makes keeping them economically viable. They compare favourably with the Suffolk, long renowned for its ability to do well on a comparatively modest amount of food.

It is argued by Ardennes enthusiasts in Britain that, because of their relatively small size, they are more suitable for agriculture field work than their taller British counterparts, such as the Shire and Clydesdale. As the secretary of the British Ardennes Society, Gavin S. Cole, pointed out in the British magazine *Heavy Horse and Driving*:

...a tall horse, irrespective of breed, will tend to pull any implement out of or off the ground rather than along or through the earth. In ploughing, cultivating and hoeing this is important as it results in the implement requiring a greater angle of depth cut having to be set than would be needed with a lower angle of draught. Thus the taller the animal, the greater the power/weight needed to haul the implement through the ground – a waste of energy and a greater strain on the horse. The draught chain on the tall horse could, of course, be lengthened, thus reducing the angle of draught, but this involves the control point being further away from the horse's head and can result in difficult conditions arising during awkward turns and manoeuvres. The resultant greater caution needed can mean much in time lost and a reduction in productivity.

The Ardennes is also noted for its agility and sure-footedness – remarkable in so bulky an animal – which make it ideal for use in hilly fields that are inaccessible to tractors.

The French Ardennes Breed Society is very strict indeed about the horses it accepts for registration (the stud book was started in 1929). All are inspected at three years of age for conformation and, most especially, for temperament. Any animal that shows any signs of vice or poor temperament is barred and quickly finds its way to the 'meat man'. The Ardennes horse is thus selectively bred for a docile temperament for working and, inevitably in Europe, it is also bred on a large scale for meat production. It is interesting that the Ardennes Society is just as particular about the quality of animal bred for the latter as that bred for work, and indeed no distinction is made when assessing animals for registration. This high standard is encouraged by the French government which, at the annual shows, buys top quality stallions. These are then made available for stud purposes at a modest fee that gives small breeders access to good breeding stock they might otherwise not be able to afford.

Because of the importance of the meat trade in the continued existence of a number of European breeds, it is perhaps appropriate to examine the factors that are taken into account when the animals are bred for meat.

In the case of the Ardennes, they are regarded exactly as a farmer regards sheep and cattle, and large herds are maintained. A farmer may have 90 to 100 horses, probably kept – at least in bad weather – in barns without any partitions, which means that a docile temperament is essential. The breeders are well aware of the fact that, rather surprisingly perhaps, about 80 per cent of horse-meat consumed in France is imported, and they have therefore taken steps to analyse their own position and to plan for a larger share of the market in the future.

They looked first at the overall fertility of the horses, and found that, on average, one foal was weaned for every two mares put to a stallion – while during the same time, their beef-producing Charollais competitors weaned eight

The solid strength of an Ardennes stallion. This is one of the oldest breeds of heavy horse, mentioned in the writings of Herodotus and Julius Caesar.

calves for every ten cows served. In the old days, when the mare also worked on the farm, she was probably paying for her keep – but under present conditions this scarcely applies. Studies are therefore taking place, with the aid of the State Stud Farm's administration, to improve fertility.

The breeders, under the aegis of the breed society, have been considering the breed standard for a number of years, and have reached the conclusion that a less massive animal will give better results in terms of meat production, precocity (early development and maturity is obviously important) and fertility.

To return, on a happier note, to the event with which this account of the French Ardennes began – the annual show at Vittel. There is a great variety of classes, including a newly instituted one for the presentation of youngstock, but the most spectacular are those for family groups. The stallion from a stud, together with some of his mares and their progeny of the last three or four years, are presented in a line of ten or twelve animals and are judged for success of breeding. There are also classes for individual animals, and for mares and foals. The French are noted realists and this perhaps is the reason for their insistence that a mare must be accompanied into the ring by her foal, which must run loose and not be led. It is one sure way of proving that the foal really does belong to the mare and is not one 'borrowed' for the occasion.

Another spectacular display, which could almost rival the wonderful sight of twenty-two horses in line, is the presentation of four horses in long reins, first at the walk and then at the trot, which are driven between groups of other horses spaced about 10 m. apart.

The Ardennes breeders pride themselves on the docility and calm temperament of their horses, and this was tested at a recent show by the unexpected arrival of a free-fall parachutist in their midst. Not a single horse so much as turned a hair.

Turning to the Belgian Ardennes, whose breed society, The Royal Society of Ardennais Heavy Horses, is registered with the Royal Belgian Heavy Horse Society, I have pointed out that they differ from the French only in size. Their breeders are proud of their horses' achievements, not least in the show ring, and are careful to point out that these successes are by *Belgian* Ardennes. The successes began as early as 1889 when, at the international show in Paris (judged by a jury of seven, of whom six were French), Belgian Ardennes won seventeen of the eighteen awards. At the famous international competition in Vincennes in 1900, when the Belgian Ardennes were incorporated into a mixed class of French heavies, there were thirty-seven French horses and twenty-eight Belgian Ardennes – and the latter took twenty-two of the twenty-four prizes, with the great stallion Spirou being declared the individual international champion. In Milan, for twenty years from 1906, the same kind of success was enjoyed.

The Belgian breeders are also proud of their breed's influence on their French counterparts when they were introduced into the French lines to increase the size. As has been noted, the French breeders were less than happy with some of the side-effects of these crosses.

The Belgian breeders were instrumental in modifying the conformation of the older type of Ardennes – horses which were described as having a small, square, lean, dry head, a straight neck, high withers, a sloping croup, legs with a little feathering, and steep hooves. The height was from 13.3 to 15 hands (139.7 to 152.4 cm.). This rather unattractive picture has altered considerably, and today's horse is clearly better proportioned and more suited to heavy draught work than its predecessor. As in France, great emphasis is placed on temperament, which is quiet and gentle, but the horse is also full of life and vigour. The breed is still used for farm work, on much the same type of land as in France.

The Royal Society of Ardennais Heavy Horses was founded at Libramont in 1926, and is responsible for the stud book, which appears annually. Ever since its formation the Society has held an annual show for the breed at Libramont, where generous prizes are available for breeders, especially those who have made special efforts to improve the breed. In 1981, 339 horses competed in eighteen classes. Also in 1981, seventy-one stallions passed the strict selection tests and were registered.

The Belgian Ardennes is regarded as a variety of the Belgian Heavy Horse, but the Society insists that it is not possible to confuse the two breeds. Rather unkindly, the Society describes the Belgian as being a heavy and somewhat phlegmatic animal, which can be distinguished from the Ardennes by the latter's smaller height and more expressive head. The Ardennes should be as long as it is tall, i.e., square in outline, whereas the Belgian is more rectangular.

Both Belgian and French Ardennes have been widely used in the foundation and the improvement of other breeds of heavy horses. For instance, they have played a part in the development of the Breton, Dutch Draught, Murakozi, Russian, Soviet and Lithuanian breeds. The breed has been exported to many countries and has been most notably successful in Sweden. Belgian Ardennes were exported to that country at least 100 years ago, and were crossed with the native Swedish horse. The cross was very successful; further Belgian Ardennes stallions were imported and, within a short space of time, a definite type of Swedish Ardennes was established, which bred true. The breed varies in size according to the region in which it is bred (as in France) with the smaller type emerging from the more hostile environment of the mountainous regions. The Swedish Ardennes has been used extensively for farming, although the demand is, as elsewhere, declining.

Ardennes mare and stallion in tandem to a flat cart.

The Australian Draught

To say that the draught horses of the early days of Australian settlement were the 'unsung heroes of the outback' is no exaggeration. In appalling conditions of drought, flood, and duststorm, they hauled stores, timber, wool, wheat and minerals; they helped construct the roads and the giant tanks or dams to store precious water; and they pulled the ploughs that dug the drains to carry that scarce commodity through the parched country of the 'backblocks'. They toiled in the south in temperatures approaching freezing, and in the north when the thermometer topped 120 F. (48.9 C.). Without them the outback could not have been settled and, once settled, it could not have been worked.

Subsequent chapters deal with the history of the individual breeds – the Shires, the Clydesdales, and the Percherons – in the making of Australia. This chapter is devoted to the contribution made by heavy horses in general – pure-bred and cross-bred – and how, over the last 100 years, the Clydes, the Shires, the Percherons, and a few Suffolks, have bred and interbred to become what is now being recognised as the Australian Draught Horse.

Much has been written about the history of Australia, and of the men who opened up that vast country. But because horses were the accepted means of transport in those days, they have been taken for granted, and little attention has been focussed on them. Fortunately, however, in 1977 an Australian writer, Douglas Harris, an 'outback' man all his life, filled in some of the gaps in a small book entitled *The Teams of the Blacksoil Plains* in which he pays tribute to the draught animals (and their drivers) in the Riverina area of southern New South Wales – that area bounded in the south by the great Murray River, and through whose plains also run the Lachlan, the Murrumbidgee and the Edward Rivers.

It was (and still is) sheep and wheat country, and the land of the huge stations, in which a 75,000-acre property is not considered large. It consists in the main of miles of flat, blacksoil plain, broken by the occasional clump of gum or box trees: country that is baked hard in the blazing sun of summer and drought, and was, in the old days, reduced to black, boggy morasses in the rainy season. Although the outback country of Australia varies enormously from

A team of true Australian Draught horses bore drain-delving. The blood lines in Australia run back to 1865.

Above   The 'unsung heroes of the outback'. Draught horses at work in Australia.

Opposite top   An evocative turn-of-the-century picture of an outback family complete with horse and dog.

region to region, the work of those early horses was much the same.

The early settlers had their own horses and carts, but from about the middle of the 19th century right up to the 1920s, much of the transport was provided by professional teamsters – tough, adaptable and resilient men, with their teams of tough, adaptable and resilient horses. The teamsters chose or bred their horses to suit their needs. Some liked the long-legged Shires or Clydes, others preferred the shorter-legged Percherons or Suffolks, but in general they were not much concerned with the niceties of pedigree, and cross-bred widely to produce the horse for the job in hand.

Most of the teamsters had contracts to take stores out to the stations on their four-wheeled iron-shod wagons, and on the return journey they would bring in loads of the great bales of wool to towns such as Hay, on the Murrumbidgee, where it was transferred to river steamers to be taken down to the nearest railhead. When the Hay station opened up in the 1880s, up to 400 draught horses could be seen at any one time, waiting unharnessed in the yards for their wagons to be unloaded.

The round trip to the stations and back could be anything up to 400 or so miles, and in the summer much of this would be undertaken in the early morning to avoid the shimmering heat of midday. With their teams of up to twenty-four horses, the teamsters made between 12 and 15 miles a day, after which the horses were watered and turned out to graze until the next morning. More often than not there was no paddock to loose them in, and at dawn they were rounded up with the help of the teamster's 'heeler' dog, who dealt with wayward animals by darting in and nipping their heels, and immediately dropping flat on the ground to avoid being kicked.

In good weather a teamster and his horses would probably travel alone, but in the rainy season they nearly always set out in pairs. At the best of times there were no roads for the horses to travel – just rough tracks, with cart ruts 2 ft. (0.6 m.) deep, gouged out by countless teams over the years. In the rainy season these tracks became a deep, black bog, interspersed with swamp patches, and their width was often extended to 100 yd. (90 m.) or more as the wagons tried to find a solid way through. Getting bogged was an occupational hazard, and when this happened to one team, the second teamster would hitch his team on to the one that was bogged, and all forty or forty-eight horses would heave and strain until the glutinous mud released the vehicle. Hence two teams travelled together.

Capsizes, too, were commonplace, and when a wagon had been piled high with bulky bales of wool the difficulties were enormous. The bales had to be unloaded and taken to dry ground; the horses then pulled the wagon back on its wheels and out on to the dry, and then helped to load the wool again. This was done by placing two poles or skids against the side of the wagon, and using two horses to pull the bales up the skids on to the wagon top. As might be imagined, journeys made under these conditions took a long time, and the horses needed frequent rests from the heavy work – made even heavier by the fact that the wheels of the wagons constantly became completely seized up with mud, which had to be dug out. One pair of teamsters told of a journey of 45 miles that took a fortnight, and another group of three teams managed just $1\frac{1}{2}$ miles a day.

Crossing rivers and creeks also presented its own

problems, and at times during the rainy season mile upon mile of country could be totally under water. A teamster described to Douglas Harris how he crossed the Piccaninny Creek in 1930:

The Piccaninny Creek, between Boonoke and Deniliquin was belly deep on the horses so we could only take over a light load of wool, with every horse pulling his weight. On the Deniliquin side of the creek, we loaded some waiting wagons. The tracks in the creek became very cut up and deep, and we needed a large team of horses to pull the wagon. Pulling the wagon up the bank on the Deniliquin side was the hardest part, but even pulling through the creek, all the horses were straining.

Sometimes when a load of stores was delivered to a station there would be no wool for carting back, so the teamster and his horses would be employed in sinking the giant 'tanks' or dams used for water storage. The horses, up to eleven teams at a time, were hitched to the great metal scoops which the men handled to excavate as much as 10,000 cu. ft. (280 cu. m.) of earth. In the dry season, the teams might be used for cleaning out existing tanks. The wagons, pulled by the faithful draughters, also plodded steadily round the stations, carting fencing materials, or parts for the many mills being set up, and some carted copper ore from the mines.

From the early 1900s, the horses were used for working on what passed as roads in the outback – or at least on those sections of the tracks that were being built up to make them something approaching passable. The horses' work in this consisted of pulling a very heavy single-furrow plough with a long beam. Indeed, so heavy did the implement become in areas of clogging clay soil that a team of six or eight horses harnessed abreast was needed. When the road surface had been ploughed and then flattened (often manually with spades), the horses were hitched to a wooden scraper to put the final levelling touches.

Log-hauling from some of the forests in the region was one of the jobs which required skill and split-second obedience from the horses in addition to their usual draught power. It took about a year to train them, as they had to learn to pull as hard as they could to drag the logs up the skids leaning against the side of the wagon, and then to stop pulling absolutely instantaneously as the log rolled off the skids on to the wagon – otherwise the whole vehicle plus its load would capsize. A team of horses operated each end of a wagon.

Much of the work in outback Australia was concerned with water – finding it, storing it, and drawing it from the underground artesian wells. Inevitably, the horses were employed in most of this, and a number were used as 'whim' horses. The whim was a wooden structure, on which was a large wooden drum that was turned by a horse walking around a circular track some 30 ft. (9 m.) in diameter. Two 30-gallon (136.4 l.) iron buckets were attached to the drum by wire ropes, and these were pulled up and down the well – one bucket filling as the other was emptying into a tank. As the bucket emptied, the horse had to turn and go round the circle in the opposite direction and, being creatures of habit, they soon learned to turn by themselves when they heard the sound of the water running out. Whim horses normally worked one day on and one day off.

One of the more unusual tasks that befell one team of draught horses in those early days was the removal of a house from one town to another. The house was jacked up on small wheels, and began its slow journey pulled by two teams of twelve bullocks. They, however, were not enough, and a team of twelve horses was hitched on and together the twenty-four bullocks and twelve horses pulled the house to its new site.

The horses were expected to pull very heavy loads, and the teamsters were proud of their animals' ability. It could be said that pulling matches had their Australian origins then, to be revived, in a different form, in the 1970s. Douglas Harris describes a feat of pulling performed by two horses with a load of wheat:

After a long day's haul with the team, the teamsters often called in to the pub at Carrathool, to yarn over a few beers, or boast about their exceptional horses. One year, a teamster with a load of one hundred four-bushel bags of wheat, weighing approximately ten tons, was camped there one weekend waiting for the railway to open on the Monday. While yarning to some dozen fellow teamsters in the pub, he bet them a fiver that he could move his load fifteen feet with only two horses. The bet was immediately taken up, and on the Sunday, he spent all morning testing his big chains and his shaft gear.

On the Monday morning a large crowd turned up to watch the event, and with relatively little effort his two horses moved the load the required distance. Moving the wagon was a remarkable feat for the two horses, for over the weekend the wagon would have sunk at least an inch, and while the wagon unladen weighed three tons three hundredweight, with its load, the two horses had to pull a total load of thirteen tons.

Although the need for horses was gradually overtaken by mechanisation – in some areas not until well unto the 1930s – some of the work done by horses in the old days is still, in a few instances, performed by their descendants today. One of these is the heavy draught work known as 'bore drain delving'. Throughout vast areas of outback Australia there are quantities of underground water which is brought to the surface by drilling bores. From these boreholes, the water has been channelled in thousands upon thousands of miles of drains. The drains need to be cleaned out and de-silted every year, and until the days of the tractor this was, of course, done by horses. But some station owners have kept on their drain-delving horse teams, and on one property in western New South Wales, the horses doing this job today can trace their breeding back to horses doing that same type of work in 1865.

During the 1940s and 1950s in Australia – rather later than in some other countries – many thousands of redundant horses were being 'dogged', that is, they were being put down and sold for dog meat. Some of the best Australian draught horses ended their lives in this sad way. Luckily, however, a few people kept their favourite heavy horses, and a few stations kept their working teams.

Although there has been a Clydesdale Stud Book in Australia for many years, the only other form of registration until quite recently was a Draught Horse Stud Book that was started in 1912, but ceased through lack of support

Opposite An Australian Draught stallion in a ploughing competition at an Australian heavy horse field day in 1980.

Right A rare early horse-drawn convict transporter, which was used for moving convicts between jails.

the following year. In its brief existence this book catered for all the breeds then found in Australia – Shire, Clydesdale, Percheron and Suffolk.

In the succeeding years, as has been recounted, less attention was paid to pedigree than to usefulness, and the modern Australian draught horse has tended to be a mixture of all the original breeds, with no planned breeding programmes and the consequent loss of good stock. This worried the new generation of breeders, who appreciated the difficulties facing any breed that has no official form of registration. In 1979 a public meeting, called by Mr Mal Frail, was held in New South Wales and the Australian Draught Horse Stud Book Society was formed to encourage the breeding, working and showing of heavy horses throughout Australia.

It will become clear that the Australian Draught Horse is not yet a breed in the generally accepted meaning of that word, but if the aims and conditions of entry into the stud book are pursued, it seems likely that, in due course, a true breed will emerge. At the moment, horses are accepted into the stud book depending on their suitability as draught horses, rather than on their conforming to a definite breed type as such, as will be apparent when the preamble to the breed standard is read.

If a member wishes to have a horse classified, the horse must first be submitted to a classification panel consisting of from three to five classifiers who travel all over the country. When a horse is accepted, its pedigree (or its pedigree as far as it is known) is recorded, photographs are taken, and it is then branded A D on the near-side rump. The photographs and the pedigree are recorded for future reference. Stallions must, in addition, have a veterinary certificate stating soundness and freedom from recognisable hereditary fault. At any time in the future should a stallion throw foals with hereditary faults, he can be de-registered. The Stud Book Society has had problems in finding suitable quality stallions, and in a number of cases has accepted Clydesdale and Percheron stallions that meet the stud book requirements.

The Society's preamble to the breed standard explains the position:

What must be kept in mind is that the Australian Draught Horse has evolved over the years as a result of the cross breeding of the four recognised pure breeds of Draught Horses and in some cases this cross breeding is still being carried out to-day to produce working horses. As a result of this the Australian Draught Horse will carry characteristics of the pure breeds; as well as this there are a percentage of them who would be carrying characteristics of the old type shire horse that was imported into Australia late last century and the early part of this century. This horse has passed on exceptionally good chest and muscle qualities along with the good heavy bone, but unfortunately has left behind it a coarseness of head. A horse should not be penalised too severely for this if it has the other desirable characteristics.

These following standards are to be used as a guide for classifiers and judges and regardless of the breed of horse, the main thing is that it comes up to these standards, for example: It could be a Suffolk Punch cross Clydesdale that has thrown to the Suffolk Punch, it may look like a pure bred Suffolk Punch but this at the moment is not important, the most important thing is that it has got the qualities as set out below.

Head The head should not be too large with a distinctive muzzle and a good, broad forehead, a large clear docile eye and good alert ears of medium size. The jaw should be clean cut and show the horse's head side on to have a true characteristic shape. A box shape appearance side on is not desirable. A slightly Roman nose, while not being desirable, should not be penalised against as it will take many, many generations of concentrated breeding to eliminate. A stallion should have a masculine head in appearance and the same should apply in the case of femininity for a mare.

Neck Medium length, with a good neat coupling to the head, clean, free of any surplus fat and loose skin. Stallions should be well crested.

Shoulder The neck should form into the shoulder in such a way that there is a distinctive collar bed. The shoulder should be well muscled, blending into the chest, wither and back area with a nice gentle slope.

Chest The chest wide and full allowing good muscling.

Withers The withers should be in balance with the neck and back, capable of carrying a back saddle, but an over large or too high wither is not desirable.

Back Short, level and broad but in proportion with the rest of the horse.

Ribs Well rounded with plenty of depth, especially in the back rib; flat or slab-sided definitely not desirable.

Croup or Rump Wide and well muscled, from the side view slightly rounded to the tail coupling. The tail should hang free. A sloping or goose rump definitely not desired. From the rear of the horse it should give the appearance of plenty of width, especially in mares as this is an indication to the pelvic area in brood mares.

Hindquarters From the rear view there should be a nice well muscled slope into the thigh. The thigh area should be large and well muscled sloping into the gaskin, which once again should be distinctively muscled. From the side view the hindquarters should be well rounded and if a line from the point of the buttocks to the ground was drawn it would touch the point of the hock and fetlock.

Legs The front legs should be straight and well set under the shoulder chest area, both from front and side view they should be straight with good bone and well covered joints. The pastern area should be of medium length with a gentle slope. Hind legs set under the body with hocks set straight or slightly inwards. Cow hocks definitely not desired.

Hocks large, strong, wide, deep, and well defined. Front knees large, flat, straight, deep and well defined. Cannon bone short, strong and flat. Tendons hard, clean and distinct. Fetlock wide and strong, pastern medium length with gentle slope. Too much length or slope should definitely be avoided.

Feather The feather is optional due to the influence of Percheron and Suffolk Punch bloodlines, but this will have to be revised at a later date when we are considering the closure of the Stud Book.

Feet Once again due to the influence of Suffolk Punch and Percheron they will vary, but as a guide, symmetrical, solid, of average size, round, squarely placed, heels wide and clearly defined, soles concave, with a clearly defined frog. Coronet wide and round in proportion to leg.

Colour All colours accepted, but the solid colours being the ultimate aim.

Height Mares 15.2 to 16.2 hands (157.5 to 167.6 cm.). Stallions 16 to 17.2 hands (162.6 to 178 cm.).

Weight 600 kg. to 1,000 kg. (1,320 to 2,200 lb.).

The Belgian Heavy Draught

If any breed of heavy horse can truly be said to have legs like tree-trunks, it must surely be the Belgian Heavy Draught, which is also known as the Brabançon or Brabant. This colossal, heavily muscled animal, which vies with the Dutch Draught as the bulkiest of all the heavies, may stand up to 17 hands (172.8 cm.) and weigh over a ton.

The breed standard describes this impressive animal as having a light, short, expressive head which is often square in outline, with a large, flat forehead and a gay and lively eye. The neck is massive, arched and rather short, with a double mane that is parted in the middle, with the hair falling in equal parts on each side of the neck. The back is as wide as possible, giving the whole horse great substance and bulk. The loins are double, with a depression in the middle, and should be very short, level, straight and well-muscled. The croup is heavily muscled and moderately sloping. The chest is large, deep and muscular. The legs are, as has been described, exceedingly substantial, with short cannons and pasterns. In stallions, there is an average of 11 in. (27.32 cm.) of bone and in mares about 10 in. (25.28 cm.). The feet, as might be expected, are solid.

There is something both impressive and, at the same time, primitive about these great horses, and it comes as no surprise to learn that the breed is descended rather more directly than many other European heavies from the ancient Forest horse that survived the last Ice Age. The breed almost certainly acquired its great bulk during centuries of grazing the rich pastures in the area that came to be known as Flanders – from which the ancestral Flemish horse took its name.

The policy of Belgian breeders until comparatively recently was vastly different from those in many other countries. They introduced relatively little outside blood – rather, they practised a certain amount of *inbreeding* to obtain the qualities of general usefulness and the great draught power they required. In this sense the Belgian Heavy Draught has come down to the present day in a form perhaps less removed from its ancestors than, for instance, the Breton or the Percheron in France.

There were, of course, *some* infusions of outside blood, notably of Arab following the Battle of Poitiers and when the Crusaders brought back Arab stallions (these affected most of the breeds in France and Belgium as is explained in the chapters on those breeds). But it was not until about 1770 that an official effort was made to introduce foreign

An American Belgian mare and foals. The mare shows rather less refinement than the stallion on page 31.

Above *Dick Sparrow, a farmer and horse breeder, driving the famous forty-horse hitch of Belgians in the annual Fourth of July parade at Baraboo, Wisconsin.*

Opposite *Belgians haymaking. At least one farmer in Denmark works his small-holding entirely with Belgian Heavy Draughts.*

blood to improve the horse for agricultural purposes. Significant numbers of Holstein, Norman, Neapolitan and Arab horses were imported, and sent to one or two of the best known stations, but the Belgian breeders were not impressed and the experiment was not a success. There was, however, one notable exception. The stallion depot at Alost imported about twenty black Shires from England. These proved to be excellent sires, and their arrival deserves to be considered as one of the most significant events in the breed's history.

By the middle of the 19th century, however, breeders were looking for something which would lighten their rather ponderous horses a little. They did not have to look very far, as around their southern borders the French Ardennes was bred extensively, and by crossing the Belgian with some of these they produced the horse that in France was known as the 'Trait du Nord'. The best of these crosses made in Belgium, however, were in the province of Brabant, and the breed at that time took its name from there.

Towards the end of the century, the breed had developed three types, which differed more in size than in actual conformation. The first of these was known as the 'Gros de la Dendre' which developed in the north of the country. These horses were descended from Shires, but were nearly all bays – huge, heavy, with excellent bodies, but inclined to coarseness. From 1860 stallions of this type were used in other regions of Belgium and in France. The best example of the Gros de la Dendre was Gros de Wynhuyze, ancestor of the great Orange I, who could well be called the foundation stallion of the modern breed.

The second type was known as the 'Greys of Hainaut'. They were smaller than the Gros de la Dendre type, and more lively. They were, as their name suggests, greys, with shades that ranged through dapple, roan and iron-grey with a dark head. The best-known stallion was one of the latter – Baptiste de la Croyette, foaled in 1833 and ancestor of Bayard, who influenced the Belgian breed considerably.

The 'Colosses de la Méhaigne' – the third variety – was bred principally in the prosperous agricultural region of Perwez-Eghezée in southern Belgium, and was descended from Jean I. Very tall, although lighter animals, with spectacular, high-spirited action, they were mostly dark in

colour, with variations of red-bay, black and chestnut.

These three lines formed the foundation of the modern breed, and their interbreeding in subsequent generations has produced the horse as it is in Europe today. As in most breeds there are a number of stallions who have played specific roles and have been outstandingly influential.

The story of Orange I, one of the founding fathers of the Gros de la Dendre strain, is a mixture of pathos and humour, entertainingly told in an article by M. P. Wolfe, distributed by the Belgian Horse Breed Society. The story of the remarkable stallion is closely linked with that of his principal owner, Auguste Oreins, who was born in 1820 in Montignes-les-Lens, when it was part of Holland. His father was a stallion man, so Auguste was introduced to horses at a very early age, and he himself worked on a stud for many years. His life changed dramatically, however, when the stud owner gave him a stallion, Vieux Blanc, as a reward for his long and faithful service. By 1866, having accumulated a comfortable sum of money from the stud fees for Vieux Blanc, Auguste bought a huge bay colt, with as M. Wolfe described, 'four great pillars for legs'. This young colt was to become, in due course, the great Orange I. As a two, three and four year old the colt, named Gugusse by Auguste's friends, was at stud at only ten francs for each mare. The local farmers, who knew Auguste's liking for drink, managed to keep him at their farms when he brought the stallion to cover a mare, so that they could get *all* their mares covered when Auguste was in no fit state to notice.

Gugusse was apparently a delightful horse – intelligent, gentle and very attached to his owner. The bond between them was so great that, when Auguste fell asleep in a barn after a village fête, presumably having imbibed too freely, a farmer found man and horse stretched out, side by side, fast asleep!

Sadly, Gugusse and his owner were soon to part. One day, Auguste found his horse to be lame, and the authorities would not allow him to stand at public stud again. So Auguste quickly sold him to a M. Lefébure, who had the mortification of seeing his purchase rejected by the breed selection committee. This meant that the greatest stallion of the time was not allowed to breed at all. M. Lefébure sold the horse to M. Staquet of Jurbise, where, apparently cured of his lameness, he sired his most famous son, Jupiter, who was national champion in 1889. Gugusse, who had been re-named Orange I, died in 1885 at the age of twenty-two. The sad end to the story is that his original owner, Auguste Oreins, broken-hearted at the loss of his old companion, sought more and more consolation in drink, and died shortly after he sold the horse.

Orange I left two outstanding sons, both chestnut. Brilliant, foaled in 1868, had a magnificent show career, winning all the top prizes in national shows, and in 1878 he went to Paris and won the international championship from a dazzling array of the best English, French and Italian heavy horses. He then repeated his success in London, Lille, Hamburg and Amsterdam, and became the most famous horse in Europe. He was also an exceptional sire, and is regarded as one of the really great names of the breed.

Opposite   A magnificent Belgian stallion, typical of the breed as developed in its homeland.

Jupiter, already mentioned briefly, was taken to France. He enjoyed great show success there before being sold back to Belgium, where he was crowned male champion. He died, aged only twelve, but leaving one distinguished son, whose line is still influential in the breed. This was Brin d'Or, a big bay with white stockings. He was described as 'truly magnificent' and at the early age of four months he won a gold medal, going on to win all the most important prizes. At stud he was equally impressive. In one year he sired no fewer than thirty fillies from sixty-seven mares. He died, at the tragically early age of ten, in 1903.

The Belgian breed, in common with all breeds in Europe, suffered badly in the First World War, during which the Germans requisitioned the best animals for military service. Of a total horse population of some 110,000, around 20,000 were taken. After the war ended, reconstructing the breed was a formidable task. That it was accomplished was due to the skilled dedication of the breeders; so successful were they that the period between the two World Wars was generally regarded as the 'golden age' of the Belgian breed.

Probably the most influential stallion of that period was Albion d'Hor, widely regarded as the horse who, by siring so many champions, put the breed back on its feet again. He was national champion in 1923, and also acclaimed as 'universal champion' in Milan in the same year. His prepotency was such that the present dominance of roans in the breed is attributed to him.

Movement of horses across national frontiers in Europe has never been difficult, and it is not surprising that Belgians were used in nearby countries, such as France and, slightly further afield, in Denmark. The first Belgian stallion, Briliand 2156, was imported into Denmark in 1895 as a ten-year-old, but he made little impression. In 1913 Belgian mares were imported, and some more stallions, who were used chiefly on Jutland mares. In 1930 appreciable numbers of Belgian stallions and foals arrived in Denmark and, by 1940, they and their descendants were covering some 44,000 mares. But again war intervened: breeding almost ceased, many foals were slaughtered and, after the war, mechanisation played its usual role; few farmers remained faithful to old farming methods.

Happily, interest in heavy horses is reviving in Denmark (the Jutland breed is in great heart) and some farmers are once again finding they are economically viable. One farmer who never ceased to use Belgians is Mr Frederik Olsen, who farms his 62.5 acres entirely with Belgians. He has sufficient land on which to graze them during the summer, and during the winter he feeds them corn (3 to 6 kg. per day) together with straw, hay and sugar beet.

More Danes are becoming interested in the breed as 'hobby horses', mostly for recreational driving, although in the very wet winters they are often used for forestry work. There are about thirty-seven stallions and 500 mares registered in Denmark, most descended from the early imports, but in recent years outside blood has been imported to dilute the tendency towards inbreeding.

At about the time that the Belgian Heavy Horse Society was founded in Brussels in 1886, the first Belgian heavies were crossing the Atlantic to America. They were imported by Dr A. G. Hoorebeke of Illinois, and by the end of the century large numbers were arriving. Their popularity was rather slow in growing, chiefly because the Americans found them a little coarse in appearance, with short necks, poor feet, round bone and various other faults. Selective breeding was extensively practised, to such effect that the American (and the Canadian) Belgian is now a considerably lighter horse – and it is said that when some of the breed arrived in the States recently from their homeland the Americans refused to believe that they were Belgian horses!

The improvement in the breed in America was so successful that the Belgian is now the most popular heavy breed in that country, being used extensively in pulling contests. But pulling is not the only activity in which they excel. They made world news in 1972 when they were used in the famous Forty Horse Hitch driven by Dick Sparrow for the Jos. Schlitz Breweries – the first time this amazing feat had been performed since the early years of the century.

In the latter years of the last century, multi-horse hitches on this scale were features of circus entertainment, but when Dick Sparrow came to repeat the spectacle there were no written instructions as to how a team of forty horses was actually harnessed and handled. So Sparrow did the only sensible thing. Having driven draught horses since childhood, he prepared for 'the big one' by gradually building up the numbers in each hitch, from six to eight to twelve, to sixteen to twenty, and so on. He also studied all the old pictures he could find of the 'Forty', working out how they were harnessed, and how the drivers held the lines.

To give some idea of the problems involved, when Dick Sparrow was sitting on the box of his 22-ft. (6.6 m.) long, 12-ft. (3.6 m.) high wagon, his team of forty horses stretched out more than 100 ft. (30 m.) in front of him; when he was negotiating a 90° street corner during a parade, his leaders were often completely out of sight. In a matter of seconds during such a turn, some 20 ft. (6 m.) of reins could go whistling through his fingers! A lovely cartoon at the time showed the 'Forty' going round a corner, with the driver leaning down to his off-side wheeler horse and saying 'Giddap – and Please pass it on!'

One of Sparrow's chief problems was that, when he started training, he just did not have enough horses. This, almost inadvertently, led to the introduction of a new system of harnessing the team which cut down the number of individual reins the driver had to hold. His method of schooling new horses to work in a big hitch was to put them in the middle of the team and fasten them by short 'breaking straps' to the team behind them, instead of having reins running from them back to the driver. This worked so well that he extended the idea; and eventually, using the breaking strap system, he found that he needed to have reins only from the wheelers, the numbers two, five and eight teams, and the leaders – that is, ten reins, five in each hand.

Even holding five reins in each hand creates a considerable physical problem because of their sheer weight. The driver managed it by having the reins from the number two team under his little finger and between his thumb and index finger; the reins from the number five team went between his little finger and his fourth finger and over the thumb, and lay on top of the number two reins; the number eight reins went between his middle and fourth finger and over the thumb, and lay on top of the other reins; the leaders' reins went over the index finger and down the palm; and the wheelers' went between the index finger and middle finger and also down the palm, lying under the lead team reins. It was absolutely essential that all the reins lay flat, as any twisting could pull them all from the driver's hands, or even pull him right off the seat of the wagon.

With a hitch of this magnitude, various precautions needed to be taken, and the shrewd Mr Sparrow – not a horseman all his life for nothing – tried the hitch out for the first time in a wet, boggy field where, 'if the Belgians made a run for it, the soft ground would soon tucker them out'!

When the hitch took part in parades through town and city streets, mounted outriders escorted it, in case of emergencies, and a distance of about half a city block was always left between the hitch and the rest of the parade in front. The precautions paid off. The hitch never actually did have a runaway – luckily – but quick thinking by an outrider saved a potentially very dangerous situation when one of the horses slipped up and came down in a tangle of harness. The team was stopped remarkably quickly, and the nearest outrider, summing up the situation instantaneously, sat on the fallen animal's head until the harness was sorted out, then let it stand up, after which the parade went on without further incident. Hitching up the 'Forty' became a matter of routine – but on one embarrassing occasion someone slipped up and only thirty-six horses were harnessed instead of the full forty! Luckily somebody noticed, and the remainder were put to before the hitch appeared in public. The days of that particular 'Forty' are now over, although Dick Sparrow did once drive an incredible 'Forty-eight', just to show it could be done.

America is, of course, well-known for doing things on a grand scale so it should cause little surprise that the heaviest horse ever recorded lived in that country – and it was a Belgian. Weighing 3,200 lb. (1,450 kg.), Brooklyn Supreme stood 19.2 hands (198.1 cm.) and died at the age of twenty in 1948.

Belgians are also very popular in Canada, where they began to arrive at the turn of the century. The Canadian Belgian Horse Association was incorporated in 1907, and now has over 500 members. It is responsible for the regulations governing the registration of Belgians throughout the country, and to date nearly 19,000 horses have been registered. Some idea of the present interest in the breed may be judged from the fact that there was a 73 per cent increase in registrations in 1981 compared with 1980, and the 1980s have been called the decade of the 'Canadian Belgian Boom'. It is estimated that there are some 12,000 registered Belgians in the country, and another 12,000 grades and geldings not eligible for registration.

One tends to think of the whole of North America as being totally mechanised. It is therefore surprising and gratifying to learn that Belgians are very much in demand in the lumbering industry for logging. They do so much less damage than machines, that many farmers are buying them to do short-haul work and, in some instances, to work a small farm completely.

They are, of course, also very, very popular as pulling and hitch horses, and are an important part of many of the 600 agricultural fairs across the country. As the Association Secretary/Treasurer, Mrs Barbara Meyers, points out, the competition and show ring at the fairs provide a focal point for the improvement, learning about and promotion

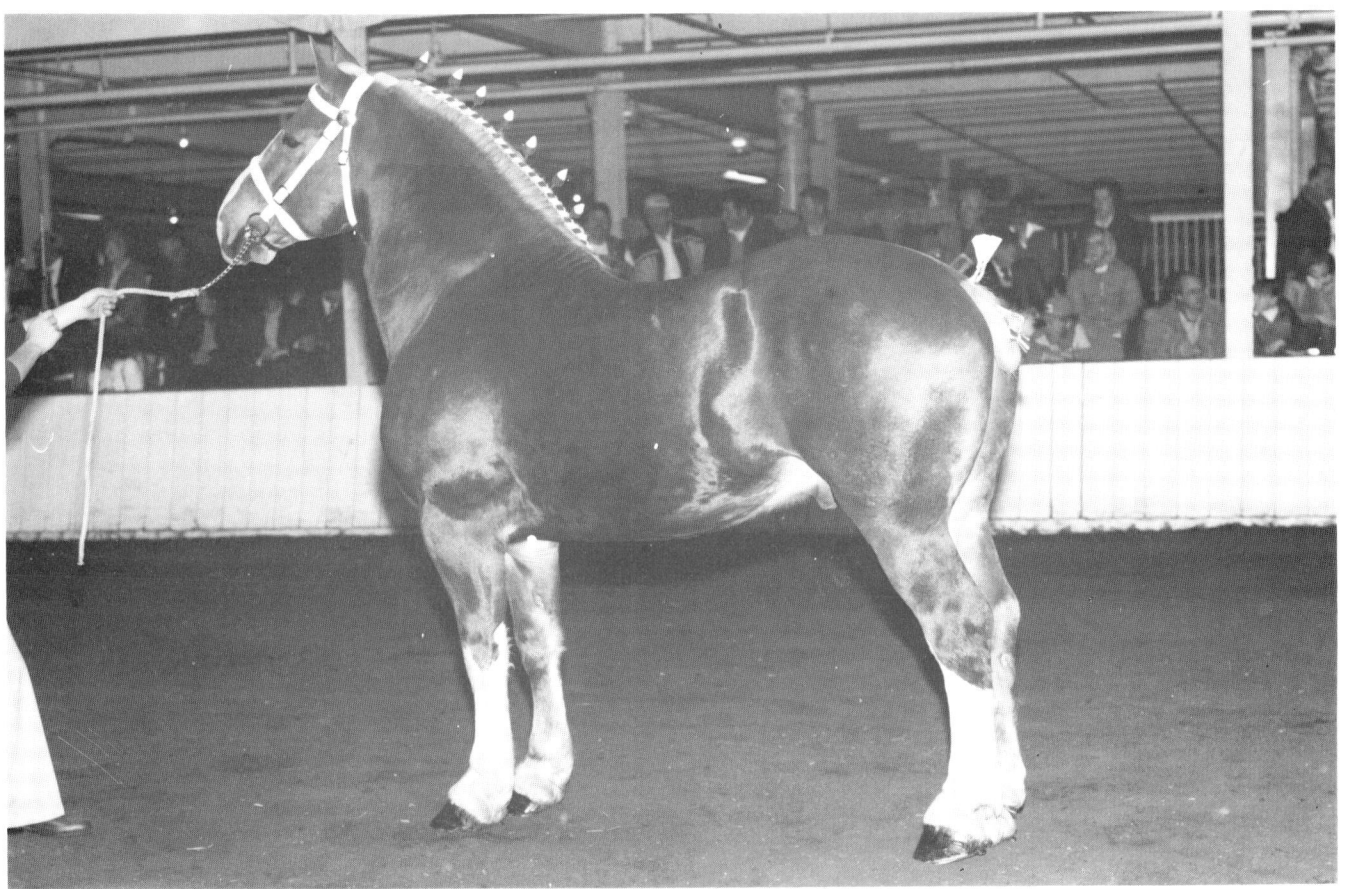

A Canadian-bred Belgian stallion. Compare this lighter, more refined type favoured in North America with the heavier, shorter-legged animals bred in Belgium which can be seen on page 28.

of the Belgians. Of equal interest for the future of all the heavies in Canada, is that draught horse breeding classes at fairs receive provincial assistance, and it is probable that in 1984 the horses will receive federal support as well.

Canadian breeders have made very successful forays into the United States, and have dominated first place both at halter (in hand) and hitch (harness) for the past five years at Michigan Great Lakes International Draft Horse Show in Detroit.

As in the United States the Canadians have bred selectively for the points they most admire in the Belgian, and today's horse is described as a more stylish, upheaded animal, with more sloping shoulders and pasterns to give action, good clean flat bone and a large foot. The breed has, however, maintained the desirable characteristics of a draughty middle, heavy, powerful muscling, close coupling and good disposition. The Belgian is still noted for being a willing worker and economical to keep. In spite of the severe climate many horses live out throughout the year, but most that are retained for showing purposes are kept indoors, being fed a mixture of grain, bran, corn and molasses, plus minerals and salt, and hay.

In Canada, as in so many other countries, the heavy horses are used for promotional purposes, and Canadian Belgian enthusiasts are tremendously proud of the Carling O'Keefe Breweries' Carlsberg Eight Horse Hitch of Belgians. This is a truly superb turn-out of eight chestnut horses specially selected for their glossy coat, white blaze and blond mane and tail. The impressive show wagon is built from solid oak and decorated by two of Canada's best-known wood carvers. Beneath the driver's seat is a carving of a mermaid surrounded by sea-horses, and the name 'Carlsberg' in traditional script appears on the side of wagon, flanked by the crown which indicates the brewery's appointment to the Danish Royal Household. The wagon carries seventeen oak barrels, replicas of those first used by the Carlsberg Brewery.

Replacements for the team of horses are specially bred, by careful selection of mare and stallion. Even so, only about two of every twelve foals are considered suitable to be team members. Each one is, from birth, tended with great care. From a very early age it has its feet trimmed by the blacksmith every six weeks so that it becomes used to the process, and also so that any improvement can be made to weak or incorrect bone structure by altering the angle of the hoof. As a two year old the youngster is carefully broken to harness over a six-month period and, if he shows potential for team work, he will be taken around local fairs to accustom him to the sights and sounds. At three or four he becomes a part-time member of the team, and at five, when fully mature, he joins as a permanent member.

The Canadian Belgian story is an inspiring one. Will the single Belgian that has just been imported into Australia (from the United States) be the forerunner of a similar story? It will be interesting to watch the progress of the breed in that country.

Belgians romping.

The Boulonnais

Of all the French breeds of heavy horse, the Boulonnais, in spite of its many fine qualities, appears to be the one that has suffered most from mechanisation on the farm and in commerce. In the 1960s, numbers dwindled rapidly, and by 1970 the stud book entries had fallen to just sixty-eight. As in the case of the Shire in Britain, had it not been for the enthusiasm and devotion of a small number of breeders, the Boulonnais could well have become extinct. Even now its numbers are sustained partly because of its suitability for the meat market and, to a lesser extent, its continued use on small farms.

The Boulonnais is a handsome, elegant horse, and, in spite of its not inconsiderable size, it is still possible to see traces of the Arab and other oriental blood which so influenced its development many centuries ago. It is difficult to isolate any individual feature as being specifically Arab – perhaps it is the combination of quality and presence, the large, bright and expressive eyes, a certain gayness of outlook, the set of the head and the high head carriage, that give the clue to its ancestry. Be that as it may, it is a most attractive breed.

It is a strong, thick-set, compact, and rounded animal, described by its breed society as being of 'herculean' build. It is not unlike the Percheron in appearance, but is less massively built. The head is elegant, short and broad, with a straight profile, and slightly prominent eye-sockets. The latter enhance the beauty of the kindly eyes, which are fringed with unusually long lashes. The ears are relatively small and erect, giving the impression of constant alertness; the nostrils are open, the mouth small, and the jowls widely spaced, strong and rounded. The head of the mare is slightly longer, lighter and more feminine in appearance than that of the stallions. The neck is thick but well-proportioned, and often arched. The forelock and mane are thick and silky. The shoulder is sloping and very muscular, with withers that tend to be submerged in the muscles. The back is straight and wide, and the loins short and strong. The croup is large, and gives the impression of great strength. The big, wide chest gives plenty of room for heart and lungs, and the necessary depth required in an animal that moves heavy loads. The limbs are strong and muscular, with well-defined tendons, and the joints flat – features with which the Boulonnais has been endowed by centuries of breeding in hilly country. The cannons are short, and free of feather, and are characterised by dryness and fineness of skin, indicating good breeding. The feet are well-formed, and if at times they appear a little open, this is not a characteristic of the breed. The graceful lines, the quality of the delicate sculpting of the blood vessels, and the fine chiselling of the limbs have been described as making the Boulonnais horse appear to be made of polished marble.

The stallions are larger than the mares, not only because of their sex, but because they are usually better fed! They stand between 15.2 and 16.3 hands (157.5 and 170.2 cm.), with a weight of between 1,655 and 1,990 lb. (750 and 900 kg.), although some may weigh as much as 2,200 lb. (1,000 kg.). The mares stand about 14.2 to 15.3 hands (147.3 to 160 cm.) and weigh between 1,200 and 1,766 lb. (550 to 800 kg.). The breed is, in fact, divided into two types – the Large Boulonnais (Gros Boulonnais) and the Small Boulonnais (Petit Boulonnais) – depending on whether their ancestors were bred on the fertile hills and plateaux, or on the more arid areas of their native habitat.

The present-day Boulonnais horses are nearly all greys – ranging from light to dappled, blue-grey, iron-grey, and even a kind of dappled roan. It is thus strange to learn that, according to the records of 100 years ago, scarcely more than 10 per cent of the breed was then grey. Apparently the change came about for two reasons: firstly, a simple matter of the tastes of the time, and secondly, the necessity felt by stage-coach drivers to have horses that could more easily be seen at night. Consequently, foals of colours other than grey were, according to the official account 'abandoned', and grey soon became the dominant colour.

The Boulonnais breed is found principally in the north of France in the area between Le Havre and Dunkirk, in the ancient provinces of Artois, Picardy, Flanders and Pay de Caux. The true centre of the breed, however, is the Boulonnais – that area of northern France abutting the coastline that is nearest to Britain. This is a hilly region, bisected by valleys and streams, and the comparatively impermeable soil produces lush grasslands rich in phosphates. The area is swept by sea winds, and this maritime association is recognised by the breed society official brand – an anchor – with which the horses are marked on the left side of the neck under the mane.

It appears that the Boulonnais breed is descended, as are almost all the other European heavies, from the Big Black Horse of Europe through the Black Horse of Flanders. Arab influence came when the Roman legions of Caesar massed in the Boulonnais before their invasion of Britain. They left a number of their horses behind, and these, as in other areas from time to time, interbred with the local stock. Although the Arabs were, of course, light riding horse types, the influence of temperature, humidity and the lush pasture in time produced, in the crossbreds, much larger, heavier animals which formed the basis of the modern Boulonnais breed.

From the time of the Romans onwards, France was subjected to various invasions, by the Goths, the Teutons and the Spanish. All, at different times, brought with them horses of eastern origin, and during the Crusades, further imports arrived – this time with the French Crusaders, notably Eustache, Comte de Boulogne, and Robert, Comte d'Artois. In the 14th century, when the introduction of heavy armour necessitated a bigger, stronger horse, infusions of German Mecklenburg blood were made.

It was not until the middle of the 17th century that the Boulonnais breed came to be known by that name, and was recognised as having two types. There was some regional variation of type. The larger, more thickset type came from the districts of Boulogne, Marquese, Decres, Samer and parts of Montreuil, while the less stuffy, more refined animals of smaller and lighter build came from the areas around Calais, Guines, Ardres, Audriuiez and Saint Omer. In the country around Lumbres, Fruges and Fauquemberger, which is not so exposed to the climatic influence of the sea, the smaller, lighter type was also found.

The breed was depleted (particularly of mares) during the First World War, as the main breeding areas were in the centre of the fighting. Hardly had they recovered from that, when the Second World War broke out, and breeding stock was scattered, not just throughout northern France, but across the border into Belgium. At the end of the war, the dedicated breeders spent long months searching the border areas for the remains of the breed, and in time studs were re-established, only to be decimated once more in the 1960s when mechanisation became the order of the day.

Prior to mechanisation, the Boulonnais, with its gentle, amenable character, and its free and lively paces, was used extensively in agriculture, commerce, and in industry. The Gros Boulonnais was used on the largest farms for carting and the heaviest work, while the smaller Petit Boulonnais

An etching of a cheval Boulonnais.

CHEVAL BOULONNAIS.
Normandie.

The Boulonnais is described by its Breed Society as being of 'herculean' build. The breed's numbers fell drastically following mechanisation on French farms, but are now increasing again.

worked on small-holdings. Some of the Petit Boulonnais, which came to be known as 'maréeur or mareyeur' (fish merchants) were famous for their express deliveries of fresh fish from Boulogne to Paris. At the present time, it is the Petit Boulonnais that is still used to some extent on small-holdings, for the weeding and harvesting of the potato crop and the harvesting of hops. As in other countries, it has been found that horses are still more economical and more adaptable than tractors under certain conditions; the Boulonnais is used on the smallest fields or plots, and on land that suffers badly from compaction if worked by tractors.

The secret of the strength, hardiness and soundness of limb of the present-day breed probably lies in the method of rearing the horses on the small and medium-sized farms where they are still used. The foals are looked after almost as family pets, and are turned out to run freely in the fields for a year or more. The good pasture and the steep hillsides (especially in Haut Boulonnais) allow them to develop well physically, with good joints, and instil a hardiness that is sometimes lacking in the other heavy breeds. This unrestricted upbringing is also said to enable the Boulonnais to adapt readily to changing conditions in other countries; in the past the breed was used in the development of both heavy and light breeds elsewhere in Europe, such as the Ardennes, the Breton, the Comtois and the Schleswig.

In spite of the present slightly precarious state of the breed, the fact that it exists at all is due (as is so often the case with the rarer breeds of horses of all kinds) to the enthusiasm and determination of a small number of breeders who are the nucleus of the breed society. They have managed to reorganise the members, and reconstruct the stud book (which is kept in the society's offices at Wimereux in Pas-de-Calais). They hold shows and competitions, and award various prizes and grants in order to stimulate interest in the breed.

The Breton

It seems appropriate that the Breton, the heavy horse which is native to the Britanny area of France, so famed for its wonderful coastline, should be employed in work closely connected with the sea. For generations Breton horses have plodded along the sandy shores, drawing carts laden with seaweed, to be used as fertiliser on the farms and in the alginate industry.

The Breton horse is distinctive in appearance. It is very short-legged, stocky and extremely heavily built, yet it moves, especially at the trot, with tremendous liveliness and vigour. In make and shape it is a very muscular cob-like animal, but with a hint of the pony about it, in spite of its size. As with the Boulonnais, this is a breed that has developed into more than one type. Today, there are three, all of which, while varying in height and weight, show the essential breed characteristics, including a delightful willing temperament.

The typical colour of the Breton is chestnut, often with white socks and a white blaze. An occasional bay or roan may be seen. The head is rather square, of average size, with a broad forehead, lovely eyes, small ears and open nostrils. The profile is usually straight, but may be slightly dished in some animals. The neck is comparatively short, very muscular, and with a slight arch. The shoulders are those typical of a draught animal, and the withers are not very prominent. The back is wide, short and heavily muscled, and the croup is broad, 'double' and rounded. The legs, in addition to being short (with *very* short cannons), are strong, with exceedingly muscular forearms and gaskins. There is no feathering. The chest is broad and deep, and there is great depth through the body.

The largest of the three types of present-day Bretons is the Trait Breton or Breton Draught Horse. It is much heavier and more active than the others, standing between 15.3 and 16.3 hands (160 and 170.2 cm.) and weighing between 1,760 and 1,980 lb. (800 and 900 kg.). Its characteristics are those defined for the breed in general, and it is noted as a fast, active trotter, often used in harness. In times past, it was sometimes used as a carriage horse.

The Petit Trait Breton (the small Breton Draught Horse), found in the central mountainous region of Britanny, is descended from the old Breton pony. Smaller and lighter than the other two types, it stands between 14.3 and 15.2 hands (149.9 and 157.5 cm.); it typically has a lively, alert outlook, and is a stocky, very hardy little horse, easy to handle, and a willing and energetic worker. The dished profile is seen more often in the Petit Trait Breton than in the other types.

The Postier Breton (the coach-horse Breton) is about the same height as the Trait Breton, but is built on rather less generous lines. It is distinguished by its expressive head, which is carried a little higher than those of the other Bretons. Regarded by Breton breeders as the most beautiful of the three types, the Postier shows great quality, is the ideal stamp of a working horse and goes well in harness. It is of interest to British horse enthusiasts, because its brilliant paces are largely the result of a generous infusion of Norfolk Trotter blood in the 19th century. It was in those days used extensively in the post- and stage-coaches.

The present-day Breton is the result of a long, rather chequered evolution, and a certain amount of more or less selective breeding. It originated in the five departments of Britanny – Finisterre, Côtes-du-Nord, Morbihan, Ill-et-Vilaine and Loire Atlantique. As with nearly all the more southern European breeds, the Breton has been greatly influenced by Arab and oriental blood, through the medium of mares and stallions (mostly the latter) brought back by returning Crusaders, notably Olivier de Rohan. These eastern horses, when allowed to roam freely in the vast wooded and mountainous areas of central Britanny, bred with the indigenous stock, and this resulted in the production of the 'Bidet Breton' or Breton pony.

By the end of the Middle Ages, two chief types of Breton existed. The Sommier, which was descended from horses in the north of Britanny, was a pack and agricultural horse, while the Roussin was a general-purpose and plough horse derived from the Breton pony and the horses from the mountains. It was much lighter than the Sommier, and was common all over the south and centre of the region, its ambling paces making it a popular riding horse. Later, the production of the Roussin became localised in the Black Mountains of the Cornouaille, and it was bred once again under the name of Bidet Breton. Further crossing with Arab stallions and stallions from the stud at Lengonnet were made in an effort to improve the breed.

Little further was done in the way of modifying the Breton until the early 18th century. Documents of the period suggest that a variety of breeds were introduced – Danish, Dutch, English, Hungarian and Spanish – and, as might be expected, such wholesale infusions were a disaster. The position was not made any better by the attitude of the peasants, who continued to take their mares to *any* convenient stallion, irrespective of its faults.

Then came the French Revolution; the studs were closed, the resident stallions sold and the purchase of further foreign stallions stopped. Horse breeding, other than in the most haphazard fashion, declined, although some attempts

Opposite, top   *Breton horses carting seaweed in Britanny.*

Opposite, bottom   *A Breton performing at the annual show at Landiviseau in Britanny.*

Above   The Breton is the most numerous heavy horse in France. Its brilliant paces are probably due to infusions of Norfolk Trotter blood in the 19th century.

Opposite   A handsome Breton. Throughout its history the breed has shown its versatility as coach horse, pack horse, draught horse, riding horse and war horse.

were made to to cross the Breton with breeds from northern France, while at the same time preventing too much inbreeding.

Little is known of the intervening period, but in the 19th century, further attempts at improvement were made, using, with one important exception, French breeds. On the northern coast of Britanny, Boulonnais and Percheron infusions gave mediocre results, chiefly because over-large stallions were used on small mares. The only reasonable progeny of this type of mating occurred in the more fertile regions around Leon, where the mares were a little larger. Percherons were used in the Côtes-du-Nord from 1890, with better results, and Ardennes were used in the central areas of Britanny. But instead of using the small Ardennes, whose characteristics were similar to those of the Breton, breeders used the heavier Belgian Ardennes; the results were less than satisfactory since the horses produced were too slow and heavy.

The one exception to an otherwise largely unsuccessful effort at improving the breed was the introduction of the Norfolk trotter stallions from England, which took place from about 1849 to 1900. These were crossed with the local stock to produce the Postier, an attractive animal with brilliant paces, which, it is generally acknowledged, has made the Breton universally known and admired.

After the First World War, various other introductions were tried, and at one time five types of Breton were recognised and registered in the stud book – le Trait Breton, le Trait Breton Percheron, le Petit Trait Breton de la montagne or centre-montagne, le Postier de Cornouaille, and le Postier de Leon.

Outbreeding was finally stopped in 1920, and in 1951, the stud book, which had first been published in 1909, was closed, a sure sign that the breed was firmly established and was able to maintain itself without further infusions of outside blood.

When registrations first began, there were two stud books, one for the Postiers and the other for the remainder of the breed, but in 1926 these two were amalgamated. To qualify for entry as a Postier, an animal has to have Postier parents and pass a performance test.

In spite of the well-known problems associated with mechanisation, the Breton is the most numerous heavy horse in France. In 1979, 684 stallions covered 14,509 mares. The breeding is, to a great extent, controlled by the government, with 557 of the stallions owned by the national horse breeding organisation.

Many Bretons, because of their adaptability, energy and hardiness, are still used as working horses – principally on small farms, and in significant numbers on vineyards in the Midi. They are particularly suited to working in hot climates, and number have been sold to Italy, Japan and Spain. Each year, buyers from those countries visit Britanny to replenish their stocks. To maintain the standards, breeders are affiliated to a number of breeding syndicates, who guarantee certain stallions with regard to character, fertility and suitability to run out with mares.

It is one of the facts of life of heavy-horse breeding in France that, in order to maintain the breeds at all, meat production must be taken into serious account. The Breton is highly regarded as a meat producer because of the high yield and the quality of the meat.

Meat production notwithstanding, the owners, breeders and the general public in Britanny are very proud of their attractive horses, and there are many fine horse shows throughout the region. One of the features of these shows is the driving of stallions to 'English carts'. The best known shows are at Landivisiau, St Thégonnec and Guingamp.

The Clydesdale

As the Scots differ from the English, so the Scottish heavy horse, the Clydesdale, differs from its English counterpart. In contrast to the massive majesty of the Shire and the short-legged solidity of the Suffolk, the Clydesdale has, to quote the breed society: 'a flamboyant style, a flashy, spirited bearing and a high-stepping action that makes him a singularly elegant animal among draught horses.'

This elegance, together with strength, durability and docility, and, perhaps most important of all, the insistence on exceptionally sound feet and legs that has dominated Clydesdale breeding for more than a century, has paid handsome dividends. From the middle of the last century, Clydesdales have been exported in large numbers to many countries around the world. Great teams of Clydesdales worked the vast wheatlands of Canada and America; they were welcomed in New Zealand, South Africa and many European countries. That they have been called 'The breed that built Australia' gives an indication of the important part they played in the agricultural life of that country in the 19th and early 20th centuries.

Today's Clydesdale is a handsome animal, lighter, and probably longer of leg than its forebears, and certainly now more easily distinguished from its English cousin, the Shire – with whom it has much in common, including a significant number of ancestors. A large, up-standing animal of some 16.2 hands (167.6 cm.) – although some may be up to 18 hands (182.9 cm.) – and weighing up to a ton, the Clydesdale has a markedly sensible-looking head, with a broad forehead, a straight profile (which, in contrast to the Shire, should never be Roman-nosed), a wide muzzle, wide nostrils, a bright, clear, intelligent and kindly eye, big ears, and a well-arched, long neck (proportionally longer than the Shire). The shoulder should be well-sloped, with high, well-defined withers (another point of distinction from the

English horse), which makes his forehand markedly higher than the hindquarters. A good Clydesdale has a short back, ribs well-sprung from the backbone, like the hoops of a barrel. The quarters should be long, and the thighs well-packed with muscles and sinews. The hocks should be broad, clean and sharply outlined, and the knees big and wide. Cow hocks are not considered a fault in a Clydesdale, as they do help to keep the legs well under the body. The legs are, like the Shire's, well-endowed with fine, silky feathering. A well-built Clydesdale must present a picture of strength and activity, coupled with quality and weight.

There is a good range of colours in Clydes, which, although predominantly bay and brown, may also be grey, roan or black. One of the features that distinguishes them most easily from Shires is the amount of white accepted – this characteristically occurs on the face and legs, and may run well up on to the body, particularly on the underside – markings generally disliked by Shire breeders and judges.

It is, however, the brisk, jaunty action of the Clyde which distinguishes it from virtually all other breeds of draught horses. It is probably best seen in show harness classes, when turn-outs enter the ring, the vehicles faultlessly prepared, the horses immaculately groomed, their harness gleaming. They show off their paces, first at the quick, forceful, long-striding walk, then at the spectacular, active, ground-covering trot. In show harness, with its sprightly movement, it is difficult to resist the obvious comparison of the Clyde with a Scotsman in full Highland dress.

It is no mere chance that the breed society makes much of the Clydesdales' action as this, and their well-earned reputation for soundness of feet and legs, is one of their greatest sources of pride. For more than a century, during which the emphasis on one aspect of conformation or another has perhaps varied, one principal has never altered – the necessity to breed for the 'wearing, enduring qualities of feet and legs'.

It is significant too, that in the *Standard Cyclopaedia of Modern Agriculture* (published in 1908), the first paragraph and a half of the total breed description is devoted to the Clydesdale's action, and the conformation of the feet and legs. It is a description that is worth quoting, as it applies to the breed today in every respect:

The Clydesdale is a very active horse. He is not bred for action, like the Hackneys, but he must have action. But a Clydesdale judge uses the word with a difference. A Hackney judge using the word means a high-stepping movement; a Clydesdale judge using the word means clean lifting of the feet, not 'scliffing along', but the foot at every step must be lifted clean off the ground, and the inside of every shoe be made plain to the man standing behind. Action for the Clydesdale judge means 'close' movement. The forelegs must be planted well under the shoulders – not on the outside like the legs of a bulldog – and the legs must be plumb and, so to speak, hang straight from the shoulder to the fetlock joint. There must be no openness at the knees, and no inclination to knock the knees

Opposite *Teams of Clydesdale draught horses working in Australia.*

Right *A modern Clydesdale champion – an interesting comparison with Grand National on page 47.*

together. In like manner, the hind legs must be planted closely together with the points of the hocks turned inwards rather than outwards; the thighs must come well down to the hocks, and the shanks from the hock joint to the fetlock joint must be plumb and straight. 'Sickle' hocks are a very bad fault, as they lead to loss of leverage.

A Clydesdale judge begins to estimate the merits of a horse by examining his feet. They must be open and round, like the mason's mallet. The hoof heads must be wide and springy, with no suspicion of hardness such as may lead to the formation of sidebone or ringbone. The pasterns must be long, and set at an angle of 45° from the hoof head to the fetlock joint. Too long a pastern is very objectionable, but very seldom seen. A weakness to be guarded against is what is termed 'calf knees', that is, the formation from the knees to the ground which begins with the knee being set back, giving the appearance of an angle which is delusive, because it is not the angle from the fetlock joint to the hoof head, which is a weakness and unsightly...

The writer might also have made the point that the Clydesdale hoof is unusually large and flat (often likened to a dinner plate) with a wide, well-sprung frog – features which were bred specifically for work on hard city streets where the frog cushions the hoof and reduces damaging concussion. The size could be a disadvantage on the farm, as it could be too large to fit comfortably into the furrow when ploughing.

The cradle of the breed is that area of Scotland through which the River Clyde runs, formerly known as Clydesdale, but more recently as Lanarkshire. The history of the Clydesdale as a more or less distinct breed goes back little more than 150 years, but certainly as early as the 15th century attempts were made to breed a draught-type animal in the area by crossing larger English horses with the smaller, but very sturdy, native ponies – a practice that Henry VIII in his day did his best to prevent by legislating against it. At that time, the horses were used principally for pack work, with the more familiar agricultural tasks such as ploughing being undertaken by oxen. It was not until the reign of the first Elizabeth that horses began to replace oxen as the principal agricultural animal in Britain. Also, by the 15th century, there was a trade in horses between Scotland and Europe, and it is almost certain that some larger and bulkier European horses were imported to work on the land.

Not until much later, however, is mention made of a specific European breed, namely the Flemish, which could have laid the foundations for the Clydesdale breed. Tradition has it that, in the middle to late 17th century, the Duke of Hamilton imported six black Flemish stallions, which were made available to local farmers to improve their stock, and although this story is now viewed with some suspicion, there is recorded evidence that the 6th Duke imported a brown Flemish horse for use by his tenants in the 18th century.

While there is little doubt that Flemish stallions played an important part in the early days of what was to become the Clydesdale breed, perhaps more attention should be paid to the opinion of Thomas Dykes. His researches in the preparation of the first breed stud book in 1878, showed that the true origins of the improved breed could be traced to Paterson of Lochlyoch in Lanarkshire. Between 1715 and 1720, Robert Paterson imported a Flemish stallion from England and founded a strain of horses whose mares were to exert some influence on the breed, not only in their own area, but over much of Scotland. They were described as 'generally browns and blacks, with white faces and a little white on their legs, occasional grey hairs over their bodies, and invariably a white spot on their belly, this latter being recognised as a mark of distinct purity of blood.' Although the strain died out in the mid-19th century, many famous horses in succeeding years traced back to these famous mares.

The outsider who ventures into the delicate subject of the contribution of English horses (and particularly Shires) to the Scottish breed is likely to be caught in a withering cross-fire of Celtic/Anglo-Saxon rivalry which, as any frequenter of show ringsides during heavy-horse classes will verify, has lasted to this day. However, there is little doubt that Clydesdales and Shires share a more or less common ancestry, and certainly some English carthorse blood, and later, Shire blood, has contributed to the Clydesdale breed, and vice versa.

One of the earliest verifiable instances of an English draught horse in Scotland was a 16.1 hands (165 cm.) black colt called Blaze, brought in by a Mr Scott of Brownhill as a two-year-old about 1780. His sire was a Lincolnshire horse, and Blaze was said to have coach-horse blood in his veins, from which sprang his spectacular action. He was sold to another Mr Scott, and takes his place in history as the first stallion to win a premium at an Edinburgh stallion show.

By the beginning of the 19th century, the Clydesdale breed was emerging as a distinct entity and in 1806, there was foaled a filly who was believed (significantly) to be descended from the Lochlyoch horses. Bought by Somerville of Lampits at a dispersal sale in 1808, she became known simply as 'Lampit's mare', and her importance is that she was the dam of Glancer 335, who can probably be described as the foundation sire of the Clydesdale breed, as most of the best of the breed trace back to him. An influential descendant of Glancer 335 was Broomfield Champion, whose best known son was Clyde (or Glancer 153). He came to be known as 'the ruptured horse', but this in no way interfered with his breeding prowess; seven of his sons were registered in the First and Retrospective volume of the Clydesdale Stud Book – and every one of them left their mark on the breed.

As was common practice in heavy-horse breeding, stallions 'travelled' their districts, and often covered mares who had been unhitched from the plough in the field for the purpose. Alternatively, if the stallion was working, the mares would be brought to him, and *he* would be unhitched or unyoked. It is said that this is how the groom's fee (a tradition which survives to this day) arose, as payment for the work of unyoking and yoking. Improving the breed at district level was encouraged by local stallion shows, and by premiums which were paid to the owners of good stallions.

In the second half of the 19th century, two great sires emerged, to whom many modern Clydes trace. Their influence was consolidated by the fact that one was put to top quality mares sired by the other, and the progeny of

Opposite A magnificent team of eight Clydesdale geldings.

Right Three-quarters of a ton of Clydesdale at full stretch.

these matings were, in a number of instances, fine stallions themselves, who further strengthened the influential lines. The senior of these two famous stallions was Prince of Wales 673, who was foaled in 1866 in Ayrshire. Interestingly, he had two English grand-dams, and it is said that his many fine qualities were due to the judicious mixing of English and Scottish blood; he in turn was often put to English mares. The progeny of these crosses were successful in the show ring, although some were criticised for lacking draught-horse 'type'.

Prince of Wales was a dark brown horse, and his face, untypically for a Clydesdale, was slightly Roman-nosed. In addition, his hocks were not considered of the best, but notwithstanding these faults, his action was described as marvellous, and he was said to 'step out like a trotting horse'. For his owners he proved a very profitable investment, as in 1876 his stud fee of £40 was a considerable sum of money, and his yearlings and two-year-olds sold for £2,000 and £3,000 each.

Of equal eminence, but foaled in 1872 at Sir William Maxwell's Keir Stud, was Darnley 222 (who was descended from Broomfield Champion). Darnley, too, was noted for his action at the walk, although his trot was said to be less than perfect and he was also criticised for having small ears; but his limbs were beyond reproach and as clean when he died at the age of fourteen as when he was a two-year-old. He was also noted for his outstanding temperament.

The progeny of Prince of Wales from Darnley mares were, as has been said, subject to some criticism for a lack of bulk and substance required in a true cart horse. However, one of their grandsons, Sir Everard, foaled in 1885, reversed any trend towards lightness. He grew into a strapping 17.1 hands (175.3 cm.), 21 cwt. (1,065 kg.) animal, and as a sire he had great success. It is indeed fascinating to trace the descendants of the famous Prince of Wales/Darnley lines, as so many of them achieved fame of one kind or another. One of Darnley's most celebrated sons was Baron's Pride (out of a Darnley mare), foaled in 1890. Although he was not shown a great deal (he won at the Royal Highland at his only appearance in 1894), he was leading sire for many years, and was described at the time as 'the most outstanding stallion the breed has known.'

Baron's Pride is also remembered for his outstanding son, Baron of Buchlyvie, and for *his* son, Dunure Footprint. Baron of Buchlyvie was foaled in 1900 and bought, as a rather puny yearling, by James Kilpatrick of Cragie Mains and William Dunlop of Dunure. The latter subsequently bought our Kilpatrick, but the sale was contested, and after the House of Lords decided that the horse was still in joint ownership, he was auctioned to dissolve the partnership. Dunlop's agent paid the colossal price of £9,500 for him – an enormous sum in 1911. The outcome was a sad one, as two-and-a-half years later the stallion had his leg broken by a kick from a mare and had to be put down. His skeleton is now on display in Glasgow Museum.

Baron of Buchlyvie left, among other progeny, Dunure Footprint, a part of whose claim to fame is rather more bizarre than that of his sire. William Dunlop took the stallion's name from Longfellow's *A Psalm of Life*, 'Footprints on the sand of time...', and it was not long before the horse established a reputation not just as the outstanding Clydesdale of his era, but the outstanding heavy-

horse sire. Demand for his services as a stallion were great, not just because of his own qualities, but because of the Darnley/Baron's Pride lines he represented. In his book *The Clydesdale Horse* Eric Baird tells of the extraordinary stud career of this remarkable horse. It was said that the horse was at the height of the season, serving a mare every two hours through-out the twenty-four hours, at 60 gns. plus another 60 gns. when the mare was proved in foal. Stud fees for two seasons were estimated at £15,000. Mares came from all over the country, with up to eighteen arriving

at a time by train to go up to the farm. A groom told of being wakened at two in the morning to take his mare to the stallion. That was in April, and the horse had already served 100 mares. To maintain his fitness he was fed on a diet of eggs, and the milk of two cows, in addition to normal feeds.

Proof of Footprint's virility was confirmed by the stud book, which in 1919 showed 121 by him, while another volume showed 146, which, allowing for foals lost, for return services, and for those not registered, indicates

Aberdeen's answer to oil wealth! Clydesdales used by the City of Aberdeen's Leisure and Recreation Department.

between 200 and 300 mares a season. Footprint's progeny were very successful in the show ring, five of his sons and five daughters winning the top Clydesdale honour, the Cawdor Cup; and he sired the dams of no fewer than twelve winners of the trophy.

Thus far the horses themselves have held the centre of

the stage – and rightly so. But what of the men who bred them, and without whose skill (and in some instances near-genius) the breed could not have flourished? Of these, two stand out, in the mid-to-late 19th century – Lawrence Drew and David Riddell. The former, who became a steward on the 11th Duke of Hamilton's estate at Merryton, showed all the unorthodoxy of genius in pursuing his theory that Shires and Clydesdales were basically the same breed (a view still held by some observers today), the differences being due, he believed, in large part to the environment.

He was dedicated to the improvement of the Clydesdale, and believed that this was best achieved by the introduction of English (Shire) mares. He was far more concerned with the quality of the animal than its pedigree (a belief that brought him into conflict with the stud book authorities in later years, as will be seen), and his philosophy may be summed up in this quotation:

> If the horse has merit, that is, if it has all the good points of a first rate draught horse – substance, symmetry, size, weight, bone, sinew, muscle, durability, and action, and if it be free from all hereditary disease, you may depend that blood and pedigree are in that horse in a degree sufficient for the purpose of breeding first rate stock or performing hard work...

He made journeys south of the border, buying up mares that caught his shrewd eye, even to the extent of returning to buy from a farmer if he saw from the train window the type of horse he required. If forced to do so, he would buy a whole team, just to possess one horse. Together with Samuel Wade of Mickleover, near Derby, he once bought fourteen fillies, which were sired by Lincolnshire Lad, a Shire stallion.

On the death of the 11th Duke of Hamilton, there was a dispersal sale; Drew bought the male and female champion horses, and set up on his own. He was, in a sense, responsible for the breeding of the great Prince of Wales. Following the Duke's death, Drew was required to submit accounts for the farm, and the trustees thought he had overvalued some of the horses. To prove his point, Drew sold a three-year-old filly, Darling, and a yearling colt, Ivanhoe, to J. Nicol Fleming. Darling was covered by General, and produced Prince of Wales. The colt was sold to Drew's friend, David Riddell, who received an offer for him from an Australian buyer, but Drew's brother heard of this, and bought him – so he came to Merryton. The Duke's trustees, seeing the price Drew obtained for the two youngsters, accepted his valuation.

The fame of Drew's stud at Merryton spread, and a colt was bought from him for Queen Victoria, while in 1878, the Prince of Wales paid a visit, and was suitably impressed. The Prince praised the mares, and commented shrewdly that they were mostly Shires, to which their owner replied, 'All the better for that, Your Royal Highness' – a remark that was totally in keeping with his policies, which by then were firmly formulated in the belief that there was no such thing as a pure Clydesdale, and that 'English mares were the best for breeding with Scotch horses, and the good English mares ran from Scotch stock.'

Drew's close friend, David Riddell, also became a major breeder and he, too, introduced English blood into the breed north of the border and, in common with his friend, was not noted for his strict accuracy with regard to pedigrees. He was, as mentioned, owner of Prince of Wales – twice, as it happens – for he bought him again at the Merryton dispersal sale as a nineteen-year-old after Drew's death. He was also the owner of the great Darnley, and his skill as a breeder is legendary. Perhaps more than Drew, he was responsible for spreading the Clydesdale's fame around the world, exporting Chancellor and Time o' Day to Melbourne, while in 1885, six mares and thirty-six stallions were shipped to the United States.

Both Drew and Riddell were, by nature, rebels, and appeared to take some pleasure in upsetting the establishment. In 1876 they decided to support a rival event to the major stallion show, and by entering eighteen top-class horses, Drew not only ensured his own success, but the success of the show. Perhaps more significantly, the pair were instrumental in setting up The Select Clydesdale Horse Society in 1883 – in direct opposition to the official Clydesdale Horse Society Stud Book, the first volume of which was published in 1878. Drew considered that conditions of entry for the latter were far too stringent, and qualifications for the stud book of the Select Society were to be much less so. The book was to be open to horses

> ... of the Clydesdale type that had obtained honour at some of the agricultural shows in Scotland, or had secured a premium at the Glasgow Stallion Show, or had been selected in Scotland to travel in any part of Scotland or elsewhere, or had passed an entrance examination by the judges appointed by the Directors.

Drew, who was, of course, the principal driving force, also deemed that pedigree would be respected and would be preserved, but it would not be a prime factor in the tests for admission, and certainly the book would not allow entry to a horse with hereditary disease or unsoundness.

The book was, in effect, founded on three premises, all of which were articles of faith for Drew – which he and Riddell had practised with success. They believed that:

> ... the Clydesdale horse, and the English or Shire horse were of the same genus and origin; secondly, that the Clydesdale and the Shire horse, when properly mated, breed as true as any horse can, of the same species, and thirdly, that the progeny of such a combination possess all the attributes so far as substance, quality, and those kindred excellencies are concerned, in as high a degree as their progenitors, and, when properly selected and mated, are capable of transmitting these attributes with equal impressiveness to their progeny.

The first book was published in 1884, with Prince of Wales registered as No. 1 and Darnley as No. 2, and the Society had some 300 members, many of them very distinguished. However, Lawrence Drew died in 1884, before actually seeing the new book, and although three more were published, and it was, at one time, recognised by the United States government, the driving force was gone, and the emphasis moved back to the official Clydesdale Horse Society and its stud book.

The Society held its inaugural meeting in 1877, when the Earl of Dunmore was elected President, and the first general meeting was in August of the same year. By dint of extremely hard work by the Earl and Thomas Dykes, whose task was made more difficult because of the reluctance of breeders to supply details of pedigrees (many of which were, in any event, fictitious) and the unhelpful practice of many horses bearing the same name, or even more than one name, the First and Retrospective Stud Book

A lithograph of the Clydesdale champion Grand National, winner at the Royal Agricultural Society's Windsor Show at the end of the last century. Bred by the Dunblane Trustees, and exhibited by Mr David Riddell, Blackhills, Paisley.

was produced in December 1878. It contained details of 1,044 stallions and 356 mares. The right of entry to the book was given to all living stallions foaled before 1875, and all living mares foaled before 1877, if they could be shown to have, at least on one side, an unbroken descent from 'the Lanarkshire fountain head'. After those dates, candidates were required to have 'a recognised Clydesdale sire and dam by a recognised Clydesdale'. So, to the ill-concealed irritation of the English, who believed it was to all intents and purposes a junior branch of their own breed, the Clydesdale was the first horse in Britain (apart from the Thoroughbred) to have such a book. The book has been published regularly since, reaching an all-time record of 6,879 entries in the No. 42 volume, and the Society itself reached its highest membership in 1922, at just under 4,000. Since then, sadly, as in the other breeds of heavies, a decline set in, and the 1981 book shows under 200 registrations and 1,326 members. However, the breed is increasing once more, and the trend appears to have been reversed.

Clydesdales are being used in various parts of Britain for farm work, and for crossing with Thoroughbreds to produce good heavyweight hunters. However, probably the most famous Clydes in the whole of Britain are those owned by James Buchanan & Co of Glasgow, the makers of Black and White whisky.

In the heyday of the heavy horse, Buchanan's had upwards of thirty Clydesdales; now they have five. These are used for promotional work during the show season, but during the remainder of the year they can be seen on the streets of Glasgow, delivering cases of whisky or transporting empty barrels to the warehouse, within about a three-mile radius of their stables. The company has found that it is cheaper and quicker to deliver over that area by horse and dray (or lorry, as it is called in Scotland) than to use a motor vehicle.

A normal working day in Buchanan's stable starts with the 7.30 a.m. feed, and by 10.00 a.m., having been given time to digest their food, the horses are groomed, harnessed up and on the road. They do a full morning's work before returning to their stables for their midday feed, and are back at work again by about 1.00 p.m. If it not possible, because of the distance, to bring them back for their feed, they are given a nosebag. They work a further couple of hours, before returning to the stable by 3.00 p.m., and are bedded down, with their last feed, by about 4.00 p.m.

When in full work, they are fed about 8 lb. (3 kg.) of oats a day, 4 lb. (1.5 kg.) of bran, molasses, chaffed hay and unlimited hay in hay nets. They have three feeds a day, the biggest being the 4.00 p.m. one.

Bobby Woods, Buchanan's head horseman, explained (with a certain amount of relish) why it is so much easier to use horse-drawn vehicles in Glasgow:

You've got no parking problems – traffic wardens don't stick tickets on horses! You can get away with double parking, and you can draw up a pair of horses and be blocking half the street, and everyone waits. You do that with a motor and you'd be in the nick! The police and the traffic wardens are good, and people are pleased to see the horses, but you do get some funny experiences with people who are not used to horses. Our 'character' horse, Chester – he's 18.2 hands (188 cm.) – was going along the street one day, and there was a lady standing at a bus stop. She was searching in her handbag, and her shopping bag was at her feet. So the bold boy [Chester] picked up her shopping bag in his mouth and was going to walk away with it – and you know, the lady wasn't too keen – she was very indignant! The thing is, the horse has lots of people give him things out of bags, and when he saw that one, he thought there was something in it for him!

During the show season, the Buchanan team appear at shows all over Scotland, and have even been down to Smith's Lawn at Windsor Castle, at the invitation of the Queen, to appear in a special parade. In their full show harness and fine Scottish decorations, they are a noble sight, and help to keep the Clydesdale horse very much in the public eye.

Less glamorous, but nonetheless of some significance, is the recent return by the Aberdeen District Council Parks Department to the use of horse power. They have found (and one suspects that they may not be the last to do so) that horses are now cheaper than lorries, and they are using a pair of Clydesdales and a cart. The irony of this happening in Aberdeen, the thriving centre of the off-shore oil business, has not gone unremarked in heavy-horse circles.

So much for Clydesdales in their native Scotland – but their contribution to world agriculture in the late 19th and early 20th centuries in the United States, Canada, Australia, South America, New Zealand, South Africa and even in Russia, earned them a special place in the history of the heavy horse.

The pictures of great teams of Clydesdales working in the vast wheat belts of North America are reminders of something that, sadly, will not be seen again. They were also used extensively for city draught work in the United States and it was said (and can *still* be said, as Clydes continue to be used by breweries) that 'The glamour of the Clyde turns an ordinary beer delivery into a public event ...'

But it must be said, as it was in Scotland from time to time, that the Clydes' biggest handicap was one of its visually most attractive features – the heavy feathering on the legs. This, with the white markings on the legs and body, was hard to keep clean in bad conditions. As with the Shires it probably did more to harm the export of Clydes, and hasten their replacement by the clean-legged Percherons, than any other single feature. But, nevertheless, for those years on either side of the turn of the century, the exporting of Clydesdales was 'big business' and they enjoyed great success. Thousands made the journey across the Atlantic, and although numbers of heavy horses did not survive the sea passage, the Clydes had the reputation of being better travellers than most.

Canada probably beat the United States by a short head in being the first to import Clydes, when David Rowntree Jr. of Weston, Ontario, brought in the stallion Cumberland in 1840, and it is thought that the first Clydesdale in the United States probably arrived via Canada.

In the States a Clydesdale Breeders' Association was founded in 1879, just a year after the British Society published its first stud book. Names such as Clark of Minnesota, Holloway of Illinois, the Galbraith Brothers from Wisconsin and the Powell Brothers of Pennsylvania were prominent among early breeders and importers.

Inevitably, with thousands of animals being shipped, problems arose with unscrupulous dealers. Pedigrees, not always the most accurate at the best of times in those days, were blatantly 'manufactured', and horses of poor type or no type at all were sent out. The American breed society did its best to sort out the troubles by tightening up on pedigrees, and by banning some of the worst specimens of horses that arrived, and this was partly successful.

While many horses went to work on the land and in the cities, others became 'hobby horses', used in the pulling contests that have been popular for so long in the States, and in multi-horse hitches that companies and individuals owned and sent on the show circuit, partly (in the case of the companies at least) for publicity purposes, partly for the sheer love of the turn-outs and of competing. The usual six- or eight-horse hitches paled into insignificance beside the Belgian forty-horse hitch, but they maintained their appeal, and indeed, have done so to this day.

The American depression around the turn of the century did not appear to affect the imports for some time, in fact it was not until the use of tractors became more widespread that the great days of trans-Atlantic trade (with the obvious exception of the First World War years) were finally over.

Although few horses are used on the land in America today, it is interesting to learn that the renewed interest in draught breeds is such that one of the best known State Colleges is running a draught-horse workshop to assist people interested in hitching and driving.

The Canadians, while being first in the import field, were a little slower than the Americans to organise a breed society, and their first stud book did not appear until 1886. However, the breed was in great demand, and it has been said that 'The Clydesdales made Canada draught horse conscious and Canada owes it a lasting debt.' Even after the end of the First World War, large shipments were still arriving from Britain to work on the prairies. In *The Clydesdale Horse* Eric Baird describes the scale of work in the 1920s:

> A seven horse team to a three-furrow plough with roller or packer attached managed eight acres a day. A six horse team cultivating with 12 ft. tackle achieved 30 acres, whilst a similar team to a 12 ft. drill of 24 runs with double disc sowed 25 acres. These rates were exceeded later in the season once the horses had got hardened to the work. Four horse teams were used on binders to cut corn (8 ft. cut) averaging 18 to 20 acres a day. These massive teams must have taken some handling, even in those wide open spaces. One account of work in southern Alberta mentioned ploughing with up to 12 horses in yoke. Later work in cultivators gave such a team a 30 ft. spread of tackle. They were even known to yoke the inside horses by their tails to save harness.

The late Duke of Windsor, when he was Prince of Wales, owned a stud of Clydesdales on his ranch near Calgary, and this helped to create and maintain public interest in the breed. But, as in the States, although possibly not quite so soon or so dramatically, the tractor and the motor vehicle took over. A report in 1936 gave the figures of horses (not all Clydesdale, of course) displaced from the land as nearly 700,000, and within a decade of that, some 18,000 tons of horse meat was being shipped to Europe.

But, as in other breeds and in other countries, the faithful few breeders remained loyal; in 1952, 140 Clydesdales appeared at the Toronto Fair – and the breed still exists in Canada, although not in any great numbers.

Although a few Clydesdales probably went out to Australia in the earlier part of last century, they were only imported in large numbers from about 1880 onwards. As they arrived at the docks they were sold, and went to the large wheat properties, principally in Victoria. Almost from the start, the Australians demanded top quality animals, as the passage out was expensive and good prices had to be paid.

Once on the wheat properties they were worked in eight- to ten-horse teams, nearly all implements such as ploughs having a seat for the driver, or the teams were driven by a rider on a hack. In the days when contractors hired out teams of horses, they used to travel enormous distances between jobs, and they would work in sixteen-horse teams, in fours, all controlled by word of mouth, with no reins. In the late 1920s, the farmers began to buy tractors, and it seemed that the days of the heavy horse were all but over. But the wheat market suddenly collapsed, tractors were too expensive, and the horses were needed once again.

Mr Hugh McGregor, who first went out to Australia in 1926, remembers that in 1924 he came home to Scotland for a shipment of Clydesdales, and sold them all on arrival ('They went like hot cakes,' he remembers) and instead of settling in Victoria he spent the next few years buying and selling horses between the two countries. Up until 1938 the trade was good, then wheat prices began to rise again, tractors became more widespread, and the horse trade declined. Since then, Clydesdales in Australia have been in the hands of a comparatively few keen breeders. Victoria and New South Wales are still the centres for the breed, as they have been since the early days. A Victorian breed society was formed in 1913, and a stud book produced the following year.

The quality of Australian Clydesdales is, according to Mr McGregor, who returned to judge at the Royal Melbourne show in 1981, as high as any in the world. He recalled with pleasure, and some surprise, that he began judging at 9.00 a.m. and the classes went on all day.

No doubt the high standard stems from that early insistence on quality horses. One of the most interesting exports from Scotland was Flashdale, a son of Dunure Footprint, who was bought by W. Moore Black of Victoria, and actually won the prestigious Cawdor Cup in 1923 under his new owner's name. A generation later, Stan Jorgenson from Victoria bought the stallion (or colt, as he was then) Roughlands Telstar, just before he won the coveted Queen's Cup at the Royal Highland Show in 1964 as a yearling. Jorgenson's father had established a stud of outstandingly good mares in Victoria, mostly by a horse called Scottish Banker; it was to that stud that Roughlands Telstar went, and began his successful career. In the show ring he was champion at the Royal Melbourne in 1966 and at the Sydney Royal in 1973 and 1975; his progeny have won more individual championships at the Melbourne show than any other Clydesdale in the country.

Sadly, Telstar died of cancer at the early age of 15 at the home of his owner since 1972, Mr Tim Peel of the Stanhope Stud. However, there is a chance that future foals will be sired by him, as semen was collected from him during the last years of his life and will be used in artificial insemination – a procedure which, although resisted by breed societies in Britain – is favoured by the Australian breeders, who are faced with the astronomical transport costs of importing stock from Europe.

New Zealand began importing Clydesdales as early as 1860, and a breed society was founded in 1911, with a stud book following in 1914. At Hamilton there is a Clydesdale Agricultural Museum, but the breed is far from being a museum piece. It attracts considerable interest, particularly in driving and ploughing matches.

A Clydesdale gelding working in the Kielder Forest, Northumberland.

The Dutch Heavy Draught

One of the most massive of heavy horses, the Dutch Draught is also one of the most recently developed and recognised as a separate breed. Although a stud book has been in existence since 1914, serious breeding did not start until the years following the First World War. The breed's very early history is much the same as the other European heavies, with some of the native horses tracing back to the Flemish; but it is not until the Middle Ages that authenticated records mention the requirement for strong and well-muscled horses to carry noblemen in their heavy suits of armour. However, when gun-powder was introduced and the style of warfare changed, these large animals were no longer needed, and they were replaced by lighter, faster horses which were better suited to contemporary requirements. The really heavy horse thus more or less disappeared from the Netherlands in the following centuries, because breeding had been dictated almost entirely by military necessity. Only in a very few of the southern provinces did a small core of horses remain which were used for agricultural purposes, and these were subject to haphazard crossing with other breeds, so that no one distinct breed emerged.

Towards the end of the last century, however, the economic climate began to change, and the need arose for a heavy horse to transport loads of materials and produce as the land began to be worked more efficiently. There then began a careful crossing of native mares in the provinces of Zeeland, in southern Holland, with stallions of the Belgian Heavy Draught breed, and later with Ardennes, to produce a horse with an equable temperament, active, with a reasonable turn of foot, and powerful enough to work the very heavy soil of the arable farms in the sea-clay area, as well as the mixed farms on the lighter soil.

The breeders worked hard with great dedication to improve the breed, and about 1900, separate stud books were started in the southern provinces of Zeeland, North Brabant and Linberg. Selective breeding expanded, and in 1914, the stud books and the associated breed societies of these provinces combined to produce one stud book and one society for the whole country, under the title of the Royal Association of the Netherlands Draught Horse.

The breed which the farmers produced is one of the bulkiest of all the heavies, with an excellent, calm temperament. Standing up to 17 hands (172.8 cm.) and weighing in excess of a ton, the Dutch Heavy Draught is built on very generous lines indeed, but still manages to maintain a compact appearance, with a deep body on short, pillar-like legs. It has a small, rather attractive head, with a straight profile, a very kind eye and unusually short, constantly moving ears. The neck is short, thick and very heavily muscled, and the strong body leads to vast, muscular quarters, which are quite sharply sloped with a low-set tail. The shoulders are sloping and they, too, carry a great deal of muscle. The chest is broad and deep. The short legs are also well-muscled, particularly on the thighs and gaskins. The size of the legs is accentuated by a certain amount of feathering. The breed is renowned for its excellent, hard feet. The colours include various shades of grey – brown-grey, black-grey – as well as red and blue roan, bay, black and chestnut.

In spite of its enormous bulk the Dutch Draught is well-proportioned and moves with active, agile, free paces. The breeders have managed to produce an animal of strength and size, combined with early maturity and longevity and – most important in a work horse – an animal that is an economical feeder, doing well off rough grazing, straw and a small amount of hard feed when in full work.

Since 1925, entries into the stud book have been restricted to animals of known pedigree. They are first entered at the age of two-and-a-half years, and great care is taken to establish each individual's identity, with drawings made of its markings, etc. For acceptance into the highest quality Preferential Stud Book, each animal undergoes a stringent selection procedure, based on conformation, and it will then be graded after a series of inspections. There are also shows with prizes for conformation and for breeding records.

Since 1921 there has been a two-yearly exhibition, where the breeding records and history of the animals can be judged. Only stallions which have been inspected and

Above A Dutch Draught horse taking part in the rural 'Ringreiten' (Ring Riding) custom in Zeeland. Mounted bareback and carrying a lance, the rider tries to spear a ring, which is about the size of a wedding ring, suspended across a lane. The custom dates back to the days when country girls used to ride farm horses and try to spear the ring of a prospective husband.

Opposite A Dutch Draught stallion onward bound!

approved can be used for breeding, and the Stud Book Association also holds an annual inspection which was instituted by the government. The licences can be withdrawn if the stallion does not measure up to requirements. The exhibition is a popular event and attracts large and enthusiastic crowds, who particularly enjoy watching the grand parade, in which twenty or thirty mares are shown in hand in pairs.

Holland is one of the European countries where the draught horse is still very much in demand, and for their particular needs the farmers find it more economical than tractors, especially on market gardens.

The breed is extensively used for pulling brewers' drays, both in Holland and in other European countries, notably Germany. In the Hennigen Brewery stables in Frankfurt on Main there are seven Dutch Draught blue roans, and the Thring Melchior brewery in the Hessen city of Lich has ten, while the Dortmunder Union brewery in West Berlin uses twelve red roans. It is interesting that with the sharp decline in Westphalian heavies, the Munich Lowen brewery has replaced its blue roans with Dutch Draughts.

The Hungarian Breeds

Heavy horses still play an important role in agriculture, forestry and even in industry in Hungary, and since the end of the Second World War, selective breeding to suit the climate and conditions of the country has produced the Hungarian Heavy Horse as a recognised breed, based chiefly on the Belgian Ardennes, with some Percheron and some French Ardennes infusions.

The history of the heavy horse in Hungary does, however, go back much further, to the beginning of the 18th century, when horses arrived with the German settlers. These subsequently became known as the 'Scwab' (German) horses. Later, as communications became easier and trade and political links stronger, a significant number of Noriker-type horses (known in Hungary as the 'Nori') were brought in from what is now Austria and southern Germany, and developed along different lines according to the district in which they settled. In the western frontier region the breed became known as the 'Pinkafoi', and in the south-west as the 'Murakozi' or heavy draught. Neither, however, was a genetically pure breed, as there was considerable variation in height and weight, with the Pinkafoi showing the wider variation due to interbreeding with horses of eastern blood.

The Murakozi showed less overall variation, but two types were recognised, both of which were, from the descriptions, quite clearly more attractive in character and usefulness than in appearance – indeed, the official description shows a horse with practically every feature most breeders spend a lifetime attempting to eliminate!

The smaller type stood between 14 and 15 hands (142.2 and 152.4 cm.), and weighed about 885 lb. (400 kg.), while the larger, slower type was between 15 and 16 hands (152.4 and 162.6 cm.), with a weight of about 1,100 lb. (500 kg.), with some stallions perhaps reaching between 1,300 and 1,545 lb. (600 and 700 kg.). They are described as having a rather unattractive head, with small, piggy eyes, a short, thick and over-heavy neck lacking in muscle, a thick mane and forelock, and short, poorly defined withers. The back was often dipped, but short, and the croup steeply sloped and short. The chest was said to be shallow, and the shoulders upright but muscular. The legs, too, had little to recommend them, being badly placed, with poor, flat, splayed hooves. Their redeeming features were their good nature, their reliability and their longevity; they were also economical to feed and highly fertile.

The Pinkafoi were taller horses, but were only slightly less unattractive in appearance. They were characterised by a large head, described as 'half reminiscent of a ram's', a long, adequately muscled neck, short withers, a long, dipped back, a short, steep croup, comparatively long, badly positioned legs, often slightly back at the knees, and with poor pasterns.

Clearly, considerable improvements were needed, and while in 1888 there were fifty-nine Noriker stallions available at various stallion stations throughout the country, by 1904 the government had provided 140 heavy stallions, and by the second half of the 19th century there were a number of well-established studs.

Various experiments were made – some successful, others less so – to produce suitable heavies during the latter half of the 19th century. In 1859 the Kisber Stud bought Percheron mares and the Percheron stallion, Atlas, from France, but fertility was poor so they tried, rather surprisingly perhaps, a Norfolk stallion, with equally disappointing results. Next, they imported thirty Noriker mares from Styria over a two-year period, and sent them to the Percheron and Norfolk stallions; but apparently not until 1883, when some Ardennes mares and stallions were imported, was any real success achieved. Encouraged by this, twelve more Ardennes mares, sixteen fillies and a stallion were imported from Belgium, and in due course it was the Ardennes blood and characteristics that dominated the Kisber stud from the turn of the century.

By this time, farmers were learning that heavy horses (as distinct from the lighter types previously employed) were ideal for their land, and, as their popularity increased, so the prices obtained at sales increased correspondingly. In the intensive farming districts in Baranya county, breeding heavy horses became a highly profitable business, and in the years immediately preceding the First World War, several more consignments of heavies were imported from Belgium to add to the breeding stock.

In 1914, Hungary was divided into breeding areas, and stallions could serve mares only within the boundaries of those areas; when the country returned to something approaching normal conditions after the war, it is no surprise to learn that different types had developed within the different areas. In Baranya county, for instance, the horse tended to be larger, while in County Zala and in the south of County Vas a smaller, more compact animal was produced. In County Somogy a medium-sized animal predominated; in yet another area, there were larger, long-limbed horses reminiscent of the Pinzgau type of Noriker.

It is obvious from the foregoing that the heavies in Hungary showed wide variation, that breeding was still largely experimental and, in some instances, even haphazard. This state of affairs continued right up to and including the period of the Second World War, during which the numbers and the standards of horses in the whole country declined sharply.

At the end of the war, there were approximately 100,000 heavies in Hungary, and although the former breeding areas had been maintained, there was a tendency towards breeding a multi-purpose draught horse for farm work.

The Hungarian Murakozi. The off-hind foot clearly shows the flatness and shallowness which is regarded as one of the weakest features of the breed.

A good example of a Hungarian Murakozi, stallion.

With political changes also came a change of breeding practices, the abolition of private studs and, from 1949, the dominance of the state studs. The government embarked on a carefully planned breeding programme, and during 1948 and 1949 imported fifty-nine Ardennes stallions from Belgium, and twenty stallions of a variety of breeds from France. They were sent to the various breeding areas, more or less according to the type of horse already existing there. For example, the larger ones went to Baranya County, the smaller ones to Zala and Vas, and so on.

It was found that the Belgian Ardennes were much stronger, with better bone, were more homogeneous, and passed on their characteristics to their offspring more consistently than the French horses. Nevertheless, the state breeders were not wholly satisfied, as they regarded the imported Belgians, while being good-looking and large, as not tough enough. However, careful breeding and the environmental factors of climate and soil have, over the years, produced a definite type of smaller, hardier horse, well-suited to its surroundings. This is now known officially as the Hungarian Heavy Horse – still existing in the heavier and lighter types, but regarded as genetically uniform stock. There are now some 30,000 heavy horses in Hungary, and the numbers are maintained by 900 mares and 240 stallions which are registered in the stud book.

In spite of regarding the breed as pure, it is clear that the Hungarians are still prepared to introduce further outside blood, because they feel that the Belgian 6 and the Belgian 23 blood lines, which appear up to four times in the pedigree of nearly all Hungarian heavies, perhaps need supplementing. Thus in 1980, they imported two more Ardennes stallions and six Percherons from France, which they feel will further improve the breed. It is, of course, too early to assess the influence of these recent imports.

The Hungarian Heavy Horse is an improvement on the earlier Pinkafoi and Murakozi, although there is scope for further refinement. They are mostly bays or chestnuts, and more rarely black, grey or dun, with thick, rather coarse manes and tails that are often slightly curly. The mane is double. Mares, depending on type, stand between 14 and 15 hands (142.2 and 152.4 cm.), weigh 1,100 to 1,500 lb. (500 to 700 kg.), and have at least $8\frac{1}{2}$ in. (22 cm.) of bone at three years. The stallions stand between 14 and 15.2 hands (142.2 and 157.5 cm.), and weigh between 1,300 and 1,760 lb. (600 and 800 kg.), and have at least 9 in. (23 cm.) of bone.

The horse has a strong constitution, with solid limbs, and although well-muscled, the latter can be a little soft. It is said that the breed is, on the whole, more solid and less demanding than Western heavy horses. It matures quickly and lives to a good age, frequently exceeding twenty years.

The head is in proportion to the rest of the body, but inclined to be coarse, with a straight or sometimes even a Roman nose, a wide forehead and a good throat line. The neck is of medium length, well-muscled and is usually moderately arched, though it may sometimes be a little too straight and a little too heavy. The withers are not particularly well-defined, the back is long or medium long, but well-muscled, and the croup is of medium length with a tendency to straightness. The quarters are broad, muscular and firm, and the tail low-set. The chest is wide, the body well ribbed-up but sometimes lacking in depth, and the shoulders are well-muscled but inclined to shortness and straightness. The upper arm is short and muscular, the cannon a little long, and the pasterns short and rather upright. The hooves are of acceptable size, but sometimes splayed, and the horn is of good quality. The legs are well set on, but are described as being, in some animals, 'as if they had been made for climbing a steep mountainside'.

The animal is short-striding, with a lazy walk, but an active trot. It is easy to handle, has a calm, friendly nature, is a willing worker and a quick learner.

A trio of Murakozis, looking more attractive than the official breed description suggests.

There is no doubt that heavy horses are still an important part of the Hungarian rural economy, being extensively used on small-holdings, in transport, forestry and in rural construction work. Their amenable temperament also makes them useful in industry and, at the time of writing, two pairs of Hungarian heavies are working in the giant Danube Iron Works.

Some 30,000 heavy horses are employed throughout the country, the majority on farms. Young horses are broken to harness alongside an older animal; after three or four weeks they are ready for light work, and are regarded as fully trained after six weeks. At three years of age they work almost a full day, and by four years, when they are regarded as mature, they can take on any of the customary agricultural tasks. The length of the working day depends on the season, but in the busiest farming times of spring and autumn, they may work up to twelve hours. A well-trained horse works without reins, responding willingly to the voice.

The Hungarian Heavy Horse is worked in breast-harness; when in the fields it is shod on the forefeet only or, on really soft land, it works unshod.

Hungarian farmers take excellent care of their in-foal mares (mares normally go to a stallion in the early spring of their third year). Once in foal they are only put to light work, and are fed well so that they will have adequate milk for their offspring. The foals are weaned at five or six months, but before this they are gradually introduced to hard food. It is a tradition that a foal still sucking should be given as many litres of oats as its age in months. After weaning, and up to the age of eighteen months, they get an average of 5 kg. of oats and maize in addition to hay or grass.

Potential stallions must pass a rigorous examination before being accepted for breeding. This consists of three tests, designed to demonstrate draught ability.

1 Walking – over a distance of 2 km. of dirt track with a load of 1,050 kg., with an average traction of 70 kg. to be completed in nineteen minutes.

2 At the trot – over a distance of 4 km. of dirt track with a load of 750 kg. in single harness, with an average traction of 50 kg. within eighteen minutes. The strides are counted and their length measured.

3 Starting test, harnessed to a sledge, on a dirt track, three times over a distance of 25 m., with gradually increased loads of 250, 325 and 400 kg., with maximum output up to a traction of 175 kg.

When these tests were first introduced many colts failed, in spite of careful preparation. It gives some indication of the improvement in the breed overall that failures now are very rare.

Throughout the years of development of the Hungarian Heavy Horse, the older Murakozi breed was left more or less to its own devices. However, in the 1960s, when the results of the selective breeding of the heavier horses were becoming apparent, and a more scientific approach to horse breeding in general was accepted, steps were taken to regenerate the Murakozi type. Thus mares similar to the Murakozis were sought among those whose pedigrees were free of imported blood. These were put to home-bred stallions of similar type and, later on, to Hucul, Fjord and Haflinger stallions. In 1972, the National Agricultural Breeding Council recognised the resulting animals as a separate breed, and issued a Classification Certificate, and registered it in the *Book of Animal Breed Acknowledgements*. However, the horses are still small, averaging 15 to 15.1 hands (152.4 to 155 cm.) in height, and a maximum of 1,450 lb. (650 kg.) in weight. There is little to recommend them, and the breed is not expected to expand significantly. Attention is clearly being focussed on the more useful Hungarian Heavy Draught Horse.

The Italian Draught or Agricultural Heavy Horse

The Italian Agricultural Heavy Horse was developed about 1860 when the Ferrara Stud was formed in northern Italy. Initially the breed was founded on Neapolitan horses from the Polsian Stud, crossed with Arabs and Hackneys, to give relatively lightweight animals, but as agricultural methods changed, the demand for heavier horses for draught and farm work grew. In addition, the arrival of heavy artillery necessitated larger, stronger animals to pull the big guns. This was achieved, in the first instance, by the use of Boulonnais and Norfolk-cross-Breton stallions, but in 1926 a stud was formed using purebred Breton stallions. A type was fixed, and this was named 'The Italian Heavy Horse'.

The original breeding areas were around Padua, Verona, Venice and Ferrara, but later these were expanded to include the plains and mountains of Sardinia. Although the military use has, of course, ceased, the Italian Heavy Draught is still used on small and medium-sized farms, and for meat production.

A stud book was started as recently as 1961, and those horses which are registered are branded at six months of age on the left side of the leg, and on the right side of the neck at two-and-a-half years, with the breed brand of a five-runged ladder encircled by a shield.

The Italian Heavy Horse is a very attractive compact animal, usually chestnut with flaxen mane and tail, but occasionally dark bay. The stallions stand between 15 and 16 hands (152.4 and 162.6 cm.), have a girth of about 6 ft. (1.8 m.), and at least 9 in. (23 cm.) of bone. The mares are from 14 to 15 hands (142.2 to 152.4 cm.), with a girth of just under 6 ft. (1.8 m.) and at least $8\frac{1}{2}$ in. (22 cm.) of bone. The head is square and well-formed, with a large, flat forehead, well-defined orbital arch and large bright eyes. The profile is straight, the nostrils large and the ears small, mobile and well-placed. The neck is slightly arched and muscular, leading to well-defined withers, and good length shoulders that are quite well-sloped. The back is short, wide and strong, with a broad, slightly sloping croup. The chest is large, deep through, slightly flattened, and the flanks are short and rounded. The legs are short and strong, with long well-muscled forearms and large flat knees. The hocks are large, clean and well-formed, and from behind, the thighs are muscular, with a convex profile. The pasterns are short, strong and reasonably well-sloped, leading to large, well-formed feet. The Italian Heavy Draught is a very active mover, with plenty of impulsion, and is capable of walking fast even with a heavy load.

Italian Heavy Draught horse. At one time the breed was used for pulling heavy guns.

The Jutland

The Jutland is the heavy horse of Denmark, and for more than a century its main breeding areas have been in the peninsula from which it takes its name. It is a medium-sized, active draught horse of very stocky build and markedly short legs, which show good bone and a moderate amount of feathering. The Jutland has a medium-sized head, with a very kind eye, a well-set neck of average to short length, a short strong back, and a body of considerable depth and breadth. The average height for stallions is 16 hands (162 cm.), with a weight between 800 and 1,100 kg. (1,760 and 2,420 lb.). Mares are about 15.3 hands (155 cm.) and weigh between 700 and 1,000 kg. (1,540 and 2,200 lb.). The majority of the breed are chestnuts of various shades, often with light-coloured forelock, mane and tail. Brown and black horses are occasionally seen.

The present-day Jutland is the result of a breeding programme begun in 1850, when the aim of the breeders was to produce a pure-bred draught horse that was suitable for agriculture. Prior to 1850 there were heavy horses in Denmark, but they were a mixture of breeds, many of them being half-bred imports, of which some were good, others less so.

The first important landmark for the Jutland as a recognised breed was the arrival in Denmark of the English stallion, Oppenheim, who was half-Shire, half-Suffolk, and who stood at stud for a number of years. He is regarded as one of the founders of the breed, and from the Suffolk side of him came the chestnut colouring typical of the modern Jutland. As will be seen, Oppenheim's descendants include some of the stallions that are now held up as models of perfection in the breed.

In 1872, another event of great consequence took place, with the founding of the Jutland Agricultural Associations in Horsens. One of their first moves was to establish a committee for domestic animals, which in turn had as one of its aims the breeding of a solid cart-horse, well-built, but not too big. In common with other breeders before them in countries all around the world, the committee appreciated the importance of registering stock, and in 1881, they produced their first stud book (or herd book, as it is called in Denmark). The stud book was for horses, dairy cattle and meat cattle, with the horse section containing the registrations of eighteen stallions and nineteen mares.

However, to obtain a comprehensive picture of the development of the breed, particularly in the important

The striking flaxen mane and forelock of the Jutland.

Horsens region, it is necessary to go back to the years 1850 to 1878, which is referred to as the Constantin Period – the first of three periods ending in 1900 which are of outstanding importance in Jutland history.

The Constantin period refers to the leading stallion of the time, Constantin, who was foaled in 1854 at Astrup, and stood at stud for some fourteen years. He sired ten prize-winning stallions, most of which were black, the rest dark brown; they were noted for their excellent conformation and their outstanding movement. Constantin is regarded by some authorities as the first stallion of the era that could be described as a cart-horse with plenty of strength, though he had a slightly difficult temperament and rather poor front feet.

The second important period was from 1875 to 1890, and this was dominated to a large extent by farmer and horse-breeder, Niels Pederson. He was also a dealer, buying youngstock, and was by all accounts highly skilled in presenting animals in top-class condition. The period was known as the Valdemar, after the stallion of that name owned by Pederson. This handsome stallion, one of those registered in the first stud book, was the grandsire of the Engerbjerg horses. They were rather elegant animals, though rather too light for the demands of the time, who had the misfortune to be in competition with the Munkedaler horses; the latter were descendants of Aldrup-Munkedal, who gave his name to the next, Aldrup period, which occurred around the turn of the century.

Aldrup-Munkedal is regarded as the true founder of the modern Jutland breed, and has been described as 'shining like a sun among small stars'. A sixth generation descendant of Oppenheim, this great horse burst upon the Jutland scene in 1890, dominating it until 1912; this dominance has been continued by his descendants ever since. Aldrup-Munkedal won the King's Prize in 1900 at Odense, and the Prize of Honour in 1905, but it was the outstanding animals among his 1,800 progeny and his prepotency that marked him as the truly great foundation stallion of the Jutland breed. In particular, he left 350 prize-winning mares and 126 prize-winning stallions, of which two were themselves important contributors to the breed. Almost all present-day horses trace back to these two stallions, Høvding and Prince of Jutland.

Aldrup-Munkedal is of quite unusual interest to the horse world in that he was almost certainly the first stallion to have sired foals by artificial insemination. When Jutland breeders saw this magnificent animal, they all wanted to bring their mares to him; in one year he covered 270, and he averaged about 200 for a number of seasons. Eventually, however, in 1901, as described in the booklet produced by the breed society to commemorate the centenary of the stud book, 'It finally became too much for him, and in the middle of the breeding season, the summer of 1901, he gave up completely, although he was surrounded by the best and most beautiful mares in the country.' The veterinary surgeons from the Agricultural Academy decided to experiment with a very crude and clumsy form of artificial insemination. A mare was found in which the stallion showed interest, and by the judicious insertion of a sponge before the mare was covered, they managed to obtain some

Feed time for a pair of Jutlands.

of the stallion's sperm, which was then distributed among the other waiting mares. Incredibly, in spite of the primitive technique, some 50 per cent of them were subsequently found to be in foal. Although artificial insemination has never been popular in horse breeding, it was shown that it could be successful, and in due course more scientific techniques were developed.

After Aldrup-Munkedal's departure from the scene, his line was maintained by his two famous sons, but the breed's fortunes (in common with that of all heavies at the time) fluctuated between the two world wars. Nevertheless, breeding continued, and in the 1930s an outstanding breeder emerged in Anders Winther, who, with his sister, ran a highly successful stud in the Horsens region. They always had a number of stallions at stud, and in particular, Aldrup, who was foaled in 1920. His proud owner asserted that, 'There has never been a horse which looked more like Aldrup-Munkedal than my Aldrup,' and he was described (perhaps more objectively) by an observer as being a really classy animal, perhaps a little slow in maturing and although a fine looking horse, had slightly suspect limbs as a youngster. When he did mature, however, he apparently developed into a very handsome, deep, well-formed horse, with good feet and action, although still lacking a little in strength of limbs. Aldrup left several good stallions and some top-class mares.

After the First World War, a breeder called Bach settled in Horsens, bringing with him several quality mares, who were to leave their mark on the breed. Agness II was dam of the stallion Skjalden, foaled in 1922. He was an exceptional horse, a dark chestnut with flaxen mane and tail, splendid conformation and excellent paces. This stallion in turn bred some very fine mares, and some of the best in Jutland between 1930 and 1940 were his daughters. An interesting footnote is that in 1978, at Tune Agricultural College, it was decided that Skjalden should be regarded as the ideal type on which to base the Jutland horse of the future.

In 1922 an important change took place in the stud book. It was divided into a register and an elite stud book. In the elite book is an account of mares which have had at least fifteen stud-book registered or listed offspring. The Society now believes that its stud book has, as regards information, no equal.

After the Second World War, the decline of the heavy horse was as rapid in Denmark as in any other country. Many breeders gave up, but once again the faithful few retained their best horses and in 1948, at a big show in Århus, eight prize-winning three-year-olds and forty-seven four-years-olds were shown. In a move to re-establish the breed more firmly, the Horsens Horse-Breeding Association (which had lapsed during the war years) was re-formed in 1956; a consortium of breeders bought the promising two-year-old colt, Horsnaes, and so began a breeding enterprise that has done great work for the breed in the post-war years.

At Tune, where Skjalden was adapted as the standard of perfection for the breed, six aims for the future were set out. These were:

1 The good type must be reserved.
2 The Jutlander must be the horse used in forestry, farming and common industrial work, e.g. the breweries.
3 A larger size is therefore necessary.
4 The hair on the limbs must be finer.

5 Grease and laminitis must be eliminated from the hind legs.
6 Feet and movement must be made even better.

Recently, there has been considerable discussion among Jutland breeders about the possibility of cross-breeding to effect improvements, particularly in the horses' action. The most favoured suggestion has been to introduce more Suffolk blood. The Suffolk is, of course, not unlike the Jutland, and many Jutland breeders believe it is a better mover. There were, of course, those who were not in favour of the idea, but within the last year (1982) a Suffolk stallion has in fact been chosen and taken to Denmark, and it will be interesting to see how this infusion of outside blood (of which there has been so little in the breed) affects the Jutlands of the future.

The Jutland itself has contributed very significantly to the establishment and improvement of the Schleswig Heavy Horse in northern Germany.

The Danes are very keen on actually working their horses, and, remembering the Tune aims, they are interested in reports from Sweden of the great success of the North Swedish Horse and the Ardennes in forestry work in that country. They believe that the Jutland could be ideal

Above   *One of the famous Carlsberg Brewery Jutlands in Copenhagen.*

Opposite   *A team of Jutlands in Copenhagen. One of the most important foundation stallions was Oppenheim, a half-Shire, half-Suffolk import. The typical chestnut colour of the breed comes from the Suffolk.*

for such work. In Denmark there is significant renewed interest in heavy horses, with driving and ploughing demonstrations being popular. The best-publicised use of the Jutland, however, is undoubtedly in pulling the drays of the Carlsberg Brewery in parades, shows and festivals. Since 1928 there has been close co-operation between the brewery and the Breeders' Associations. At one time, the brewery had no fewer than 210 horses; now the number is down to twenty, but they are still used to transport beer around Copenhagen.

There are now only 1,000 Jutlands, but such is the enthusiasm of breeders that their future seems assured.

The Lithuanian Heavy Harness Horse See THE RUSSIAN HEAVY BREEDS.

The Noriker

One of the most interesting features of the Austrian draught horse, the Noriker, is the wide range of coat colours. The most common is brown, but there are chestnuts (often with flaxen manes and tails), bays, blacks, greys, blue roans, dapples, brindles and, although comparatively rare now, some spotted animals. The origin of the latter is obscure, but the coat pattern was said to be reinforced in monastic times by out-crosses to Andalucian and Neapolitan horses. A number of colour lines are responsible for some of the variations, notably the Elmar and Helios-Moritz (dapple and brindle), and the Forstaur Hau, which produces dapple greys and animals with black heads.

The Noriker is a middle-weight draught horse with mares standing 15.3 to 17 hands (160 to 172 cm.) and stallions 16 to 17.1 hands (162.6 to 175.3 cm.). The breed has been developed as a practical work horse rather than for sheer beauty of appearance, and the critical eye will immediately note its least attractive feature – a rather large, Roman-nosed head. This is relieved to some extent by the lively yet kind expression in the eyes.

The overall impression is of a medium-sized, fairly long-backed draught animal, described by the breed society as 'rectangular' in outline. The neck is of moderate length, with a thick, slightly wavy mane and forelock. The withers are not pronounced, and the shoulders are well-muscled without being 'loaded'. The back, although relatively longer than in some other draught breeds, is nonetheless well-muscled and broad, and leads to short, wide quarters. The body should have sufficient depth, and any tendency to its being cylindrical is considered a serious fault.

The Noriker stands on short, extremely strong, sound limbs. The fore-arm is powerfully muscled, the knees wide and the cannons short, with at least $8\frac{1}{2}$ in. (22 cm.) of quality flat bone in mares, and $9\frac{1}{2}$ in. (24 cm.) in stallions. Generally, the bone should be 13.5 per cent of the height in mares and 14.5 per cent in stallions. In the hind legs, breeders aim for exceptionally well-muscled second thighs, denoting good pulling power, and wide, open hocks. Short, strong fetlocks and short pasterns are a feature. The legs bear little feather. Ideally, all Norikers should have sound feet, and many of them do, but in some animals, especially those bred in some of the moorland areas of Austria, a deficiency of phosphate in the pasture (the better grass is reserved for cows) leads to flat, brittle hooves.

The Noriker moves well, with a lively trot, and is noted for its agility and surefootedness – attributes no doubt resulting from centuries of living and working in the rough going of the Austrian Alps. The breed is also noted for its kindly, amenable temperament, its lively yet calm outlook and its excellence as a draught animal under the rigorous conditions of its mountainous homeland. The hardiness of the breed is maintained by keeping much of the breeding stock on the alpine pastures at heights of over 2,000 m., without shelter or supplementary feeding.

The story of the Noriker began about 2,000 years ago, when the Romans, in the course of their progress northwards over the Alps towards the Danube and the Rhine, occupied the area that approximates to what is now Austria. It became known as the province of Noricum – hence the name of the modern breed. With them the Romans brought heavy war horses, which had been bred in ancient Thessaly. Later, when Noricum and the neighbouring province of Salzburg formed an important defence and trade link with the more northerly and westerly Roman possessions, more heavy horses were brought in as pack animals. The Roman occupation lasted some 400 years, and during that time, inevitably, their horses adapted themselves to the harsh mountain climate, the soil and the rough going of the eastern Alpine region. A certain amount of interbreeding occurred, with some influx of blood from western Europe, and so evolved a breed of adaptable hardy, agile, mountain draught animals, which formed the basis of today's Noriker breed.

The breeding of heavy horses continued in a more or less haphazard fashion until the late 16th century, at which time it came under the jurisdiction of the monasteries. In 1575, Archbishop Johann Jacob von Kuen founded a number of studs at Salzburg, Pongau, Hallein and in Pinzgau. It was during this early period of the monastic control that outcrosses were made to Neapolitans and Andalucians. A century later the Archbishop of Salzburg established the first stud book, and in 1688, Archbishop Graf Thun ordered that stricter breeding methods should be enforced. It was not until 1703 that breed standards were finally formulated, and the breeding of Norikers conformed to recognised principles. A breeding programme existed, in which the mountain farmers could bring their mares to various stallion depots, or if the distance was too great, the stallions were ridden from place to place. The breed was not then known as Noriker, but as Pinzgauer, which was then the centre of breeding.

Early in the 19th century, some of the monastic studs were dispersed, and others were taken over by the state. Many of the stallions were gathered together in the stables of the state salt monopoly in Stadl, where, in addition to their stud duties, some were used for towing empty barges which had brought salt down from Upper Austria. This collection of stallions formed the nucleus of what was to become the present-day state stallion office or depot of Stadl Paura. In 1850, some of the stallions bred in the Pinzgauer region were brought to Stadl Paura, and this strengthened the Noriker breed as a whole.

Meanwhile, in Salzburg, breeders experimented with

Noriker mares and foals 2,000 metres up in the mountains. The marked Roman nose that spoils some specimens is visible on the horse at the extreme right.

outcrosses to Clydesdales and Belgian Brabants (now known as Belgian Draughts), but this was not a success.

In 1898 a number of Pinzgauer Horse Societies in the Salzburg area amalgamated, and in 1903 they produced a stud book with 450 stallions and more than 1,000 mares registered. Similar societies were formed in other parts of Austria and the breeding of pure-bred Norikers throughout the country was thus given great encouragement.

A number of the regions, because of their differing environments, produced their own characteristic versions of the Noriker horse. In Pinzgauer, for instance, the horses tended to be heavier; in Pogau they remained much more like the original type; in Kärnten they were more on the leg; in Steiermakr they were shorter and lighter; and in the Dolomites they were small, but with great quality.

For centuries Norikers were used for general farm and pack work, their sure-footedness making them especially suitable for the mountain farms. Mechanisation has meant a sharp deline in their employment as work horses, although they are still used on some mountain farms and in forestry. In addition, they are now used for drawing sledges in the mountain resorts and, to a small extent, for riding. Some of the few remaining spotted Norikers are used in circuses. Under most conditions, they start work at about two-and-a-half years of age.

Some idea of the decline in numbers over recent years can be seen from the following figures. In 1968 there were some 34,500 (nearly 60 per cent of the total horse population in Austria); ten years later there were just 9,000 (21.5 per cent of the total). However, in contrast to some other European countries, there are encouraging signs that this decrease is at least slowing down – even though the Noriker Horse Society laments that it now has more human than equine members. (This is largely because a number of the older members still support the Society although they no longer breed horses themselves.)

Indications that the decline in the breed may have reached its lowest and perhaps be on the upturn is seen in the market trends for filly foals. In the county of Salzburg, the years 1977 to 1979 saw fewer filly foals born; but, although in 1980 auction prices for fillies were lower than for colts, by 1981, there had been a 9 per cent increase in the price. This had the effect of arousing more interest in fillies; breeders kept their better filly foals, and also had their

Above, left *The lively trot of the Noriker is put to good use in the snow.*

Above, right *A Noriker stallion showing the typical waviness of the mane and tail.*

Opposite *This spotted horse shows one of the more unusual (and now one of the least common) colours in the breed. The origin of the colour is obscure but was reinforced in monastic times by outcrosses to Neapolitans. This coat pattern is much sought after by circuses.*

mares covered again. Also in 1981, the Salzburg Noriker Society re-started auctions for filly foals, with the best ones being branded with a Z, and consequently bringing higher prices. Filly foals in general are being looked at much more carefully with an eye to the future development of the breed.

In Austria today, the selection and breeding of stallions is largely in the hands of the government. The stallions are selected for movement, conformation and performance, with the aim of maintaining and improving the Noriker as a draught breed. It is very encouraging that the meat market, once a very important factor in the breeding aims, is at present declining in Austria, and consequently selection of stallions and breeding stock is once again placing emphasis on requirements for performance.

The state owns over 100 stallions and, from March 15th to July 15th each year, they are sent to stallion stations all over the country, where the mares are brought to them. In 1980, 111 stallions covered 2,719 mares, which the authorities regarded as satisfactory. Most mares are covered for the first time as three-year-olds. The government and the farmers work closely together to ensure a constant upply of good quality stallions. The farmers in the principal breeding areas of Kärnten and Salzburg buy the best seventy to eighty colt foals from all over Austria and rear them on their farms. The best sixteen to twenty yearlings are then selected by the Noriker breeding organisation, and are reared together until they are about two-and-a-half years old, when they are offered to the government. About eight or ten of these two-and-a-half-year-olds are selected for breeding (according to requirements) and are sent to the Stadl Paura stallion station.

There are five principal blood lines in the Noriker breed. The Vulkan line accounts for 55 per cent of the total, the Nero 22 per cent, the Diamant 10 per cent, the Elmar 11 per cent, and the Schauntiz 3 per cent. Over the centuries a number of strains have evolved, due, as has been seen, to the varying environment in different regions of Austria and, in one instance, of Germany. The best known are the Carinthian (in Kärnten), Steier, Tyrolian (Tiroler), and the Bavarian.

The latter, also known as the Pinzgauer Noriker, was introduced into Bavaria in Southern Germany at the end of the last century from its original breeding area of Pinzgauer in Salzburg province. It is now known, in its chief German breeding area of Bavaria and Baden Wartenburg, as the South German Heavy Horse. At the end of the last century the breeders in Upper Bavaria infused some Holstein and Oldenburger blood, while in Lower Bavaria, crosses with a remarkable mixture of outside blood were introduced – running through the lighter Cleveland Bay, Oldenburg and Norman, to the heavy Belgian and Clydesdale. However, after the First World War the demand was, once again, for the original Noriker, and in Lower Bavaria, at least, the breeders reverted to using Pinzgauer stallions.

These South German horses are a little smaller than the Austrian Noriker, standing about 15.3 hands (160 cm.) but they still have the rather large head and the longish back of the original breed. Many are chestnuts with flaxen mane and tail.

Another variation, based on the Noriker, is bred in Hochschwarzwald, and is known locally as the Schwarzwalker chestnut. This horse is smaller than either the Bavarian or the Austrian Noriker, standing only 14.3 hands to 15 hands (149.9 to 152.4 cm.), and has a much more refined head. These horses can be seen in the city of Munich where, decked in spectacular and colourful harness, they pull the wagons of the city's breweries at festival time.

The North Swedish

These attractive, medium-sized, compact horses are predominantly bay, but any solid colour is accepted. Stallions stand about 15.2 hands (157.5 cm) and mares around 15 hands (152.4 cm.) and they weigh approximately between 1,440 and 1,655 lb. (650 and 750 kg.) and 1,200 and 1,545 lb. (550 and 700 kg.), respectively. They have a relatively large head with long ears, a short, crested neck, and strong, sloping shoulders. The back is comparatively long but deep and strong, and the hindquarters rounded and very powerful. The legs are short, strong, and with excellent bone. The mane and tail are abundant. Infusions of some light-horse blood towards the end of the 19th century has left its mark on the form and paces of the North Swedish Horse, as these are more typical of a riding horse than of the heavier breeds of draught horse.

The North Swedish is one of the most recently established breeds of draught horse. It is especially interesting as it has, since its official recognition in 1900, been the subject of intensive and thorough investigation and testing with the aim of improving its all-round usefulness as a working animal – notably in the field of forestry, in which it has an unrivalled reputation for agility, energy, hardiness and good temperament.

The breed is descended from the ancient Swedish native work horse, and although little is known of this animal's origins, it was a small, hardy, willing horse, of considerable longevity, with life-spans of thirty or even forty years not uncommon. The Swedish horse was considerably influenced by the Norwegian Dole (formerly known as the Gudbrandsdal), and during part of the 19th century, lighter blood from Europe was also introduced. In the later decades of the 19th century, however, as the introduction of heavier agricultural and forestry implements necessitated stronger horses, stallions of larger breeds, such as Belgians and Clydesdales, were used to obtain increased size and strength.

The indiscriminate nature of the cross-breeding, which began in the south and moved northwards through Sweden, began to threaten the existence of the native horse and in 1894, the Association of the Friends of the Horse was formed. The aim of this Association, led by a veterinary surgeon, was to reconstruct the North Swedish Horse, using those animals that remained in some of the more remote northern settlements, together with the closely related Dole stallions.

It became obvious that the long-term future of the breed could not rest on imported stallions, some of which were not of top quality, and a move towards national stallion breeding was instituted by the veterinary profession. In 1903, this move received enormous encouragement when the government provided a former military residence at Wangen in Central Sweden to be used as a stallion-rearing institute for the North Swedish Horse. It can truly be said that from that time the future of the breed was assured.

Wangen, which is run by the Jämtland County Agricultural Society, has as its aim (to quote a booklet produced on the occasion of its seventy-fifth anniversary in 1978): 'By means of hardening rearing in groups, to raise hardy, energetic and durable stallions of suitable size and sturdiness, primarily for forestry work but also for farming in Norrland and for other purposes, an "all-round" horse.' It has received a government subsidy since 1914.

Each autumn, about fifteen colt foals from all over the country are chosen, after careful examination, for rearing at Wangen. They are reared in age groups until they are three years old under a system of flock-rearing which includes daily outdoor exercise throughout the year, to allow them to develop into strong physical specimens. They are fed on hay, with barley and oats, and with mineral additives and protein for the younger age groups.

At the age of three they undergo extremely tough selection tests, and of each annual intake of fifteen, only about three or four are chosen as potential breeding stock; the latter remain at Wangen for another year, stabled in separate boxes, to undergo final assessment. Those that pass the final judging are then sold to breeding associations or private breeders all over Sweden. Since the inception of the scheme, nearly 700 stallions have been approved – including some of the best known sires in the breed, such as Valde, Benus and Vlandand. Fertility records of all stallions are kept.

Wangen works closely with the veterinary profession and the Royal Veterinary College, and because of an incidence of side bone in the breed in its early days, all stallions have their forelegs X-rayed twice a year, with the result that the condition is now very largely under control.

Because of the importance of the breed in forestry, Wangen introduced draught tests in 1928. They are still held there, and there are others for stallions and mares at agricultural shows in different parts of Sweden. The tests are of two kinds – a draught aptitude test, to assess *how* the horse pulls a load, and a maximum efficiency test, to determine the actual weight it can pull.

The aptitude test consists of the horse being driven along a 600-m. cross-country track, with a standard load on a 'skidding sled'. The weight of the sled and the load is adjusted so that the resistance on the track's steepest section is 275 kg. (this compares with the average draught power of 180 kg. for a *pair* of horses drawing a 23-in. (30.5-cm.) plough in medium-heavy soil). At two places along the track there are one-minute compulsory halts, which also test the horse's obedience. The test is judged by two umpires, who are out on the track to assess each

Drilling with a pair in Sweden. The practice of the foal following the mare at work is widespread in Europe.

horse's performance, and a veterinary surgeon at the end who notes pulse rate, respiration and sweating (if any). Each judge has five points to award, and the horses are eventually divided into three classes according to their results. Time is not taken into account unless it is excessively long or short.

The maximum efficiency test is done with a braking wagon attached to a measuring device or dynamometer, by which means the load a horse is able to pull is determined.

The tests have obvious significance in the North Swedish breed's most important work – lumbering. The loads of timber are exceedingly heavy, and the country in which they work very rough, made harder in winter by ice and deep snow. Lumbering sites are often in the remotest areas of the country, and the accommodation for the horses is, of necessity, of a temporary nature. So bad were conditions for the animals that up until the early 1960s they deteriorated at such a rate that many became unfit for work after just a single season. Clearly, improvements were urgently required, and a two-year survey was conducted among a large number of horses selected at random from among 4,300 working in a particular county. The information obtained covered sixty-six separate points, including age, food, general management, foot care, stabling, climatic conditions, harness, injuries, the type of country, and even the details of the drivers and their ability.

It became apparent that the customary food – hay and oats – was insufficient for the extremely hard work required of the horses, and a diet including molasses, with equal parts of oats and barley, was recommended.

Poor management was found to be one of the reasons for the alarmingly fast deterioration of the horses. Foot and leg trouble of various kinds was common. Greasy foot was particularly troublesome, resulting quite often from the fact that the horses were kept in stables that were not sufficiently well mucked-out. It was also found that in a number of horses working on bare ground, their feet went through the surface crust and became caked with the underlying mud. This led to the breaking of the skin and subsequent infection. The simple way of preventing this was washing the legs immediately after work.

It was also found that sharp calkins, essential for winter work, were incorrectly placed – two being used on the toes of the shoes. These were causing deep wounds in the heels and coronary bands as the horses struck into themselves. A less damaging, hard alloy calkin was devised, and four of these were fitted to each shoe – two at the toe, one on each branch, thus distributing the weight evenly.

The temporary stables were found to be totally unsatisfactory, as most lacked adequate ventilation systems. It was calculated that each horse gave off up to five litres of water (more, if it was wet or snowing) *per night* – thus increasing the humidity dramatically, and preventing their coats from drying out properly. Thus when they came out into the cold in the morning, their coats immediately became covered in frost.

Many of the drivers held firmly to the belief that manure left in the stables gave off heat and so was of benefit. In fact, it only added to the humidity, in an atmosphere already tainted by lack of ventilation. Clearly, many of the problems were caused by ignorance, so the authorities arranged for experienced instructors to visit the lumber camps to give advice and discuss the difficulties. One-day courses were held for drivers, which covered every aspect of horse care from harness and hitching to feeding and general stable management. The result has been a general improvement in conditions, and a less rapid turnover of horses.

Present-day forestry horses begin moderate work at about three years of age, and by the time they are five they are capable of doing a full eight- to ten-hour day. They are fed three times a day, with young horses being given extra vitamins and minerals.

It is encouraging to learn that in Sweden the demand for good forestry horses, who had been suffering something of a decline, now far exceeds the supply. New forestry laws, which restrict the amount of damaged wood that may lie in forests, has resulted in an increased demand for horses, in fact greater than for some time. It has been found, not for the first time in the recent history of heavy horses, that they are sometimes cheaper and more efficient than the most modern machinery.

The Swedes are justifiably proud of their draught horse, which, through painstaking breeding programmes, has been rescued from possibly extinction to become a sound, willing animal of delightful temperament, contributing significantly to the country's economy.

Opposite   *A North Swedish horse seen against the background of the forests in which they do such sterling work.*

Below   *A North Swedish mare, accompanied by her foal, taking part in a performance test to prove suitability for heavy draught work. The test involves pulling a load on a 'skidding sled'.*

The Percheron

The Percheron, native of the Perche region of north-west France, is nothing if not adaptable. In the course of its long history it has been in turn war horse, farm horse, coach horse, riding horse, dray horse, and widely used improver of other breeds. It has adapted happily to the very different climatic conditions of Europe, North and South America, as well as the sub-zero temperatures of the Falkland Islands and the tropical heat of north Australia.

This magnificent breed, whose beautiful eye and quality head bear witness to early and prepotent Arab influence, can lay claim, at its best, to be the most handsome of heavy horses. It is a tragedy that, in the interests of meat production, some specimens in their native land are showing a tendency to grossness and lack of quality, with limbs that fall short of the usual exceptionally high standard of the breed.

Standing between 15.2 and 16.3 hands (157.5 and 170.2 cm.) and weighing around 1,980 lb. (900 kg.), the Percheron of today is somewhere between some of the two extremes that have been seen in the past. The height and substance have varied over the years, according to fashion or to the uses to which the horses were put. For instance, the coach or carriage horses were only about 15.2 hands high (157.5 cm.), and very active, capable of travelling at 8 to 10 m.p.h. even when encumbered by a heavy vehicle. At the other end of the scale, by the middle of the last century, the Percheron had become much more massive. This was largely due to the arrival of the railways, the subsequent collapse of the market for coach horses, and the effort to breed huge, heavy dray horses, and partly to satisfy the demand from the United States for enormous animals.

The Percheron is nearly always an attractive dappled grey, or black; the occasional bay, chestnut or roan is said to trace back to the Arab infusions; the latter colours are accepted in France, but cannot be registered in Britain. The dapple-grey Percheron is said to be the model for the original dapple-grey rocking horse.

The breed has an elegant head, with a wide, square forehead, fine, long ears and full, kind eyes. The profile is straight and the nostrils wide and open. The nicely curved neck, with its thick mane, leads to good, well-defined withers, followed by short, straight and very powerful back and loins, and long, smooth, muscular quarters. The tail is well-set and level with the croup. The limbs (again in the best animals) are exceedingly good, and the breed is renowned for the hard-wearing blue horn of its feet. The legs are typically clean, although very old horses may develop a little feathering around the fetlocks.

Le Perche, the home of the breed, consists mostly of undulating country, intersected by small valleys along whose bottoms there is good pasture. The climate is temperate, and the soil is clayey with a good limestone base, which undoubtedly has contributed to the Percheron's excellent bone.

The Percheron is said to be the horse on which the Franks defeated the Moslems at the Battle of Poitiers in AD 732. For European (and especially for French) horses, the Battle of Poitiers was of some moment, because, as has been mentioned in previous chapters, the Moslems left behind their fine Barbary and Arab stallions. These interbred with local heavier horses, producing a more agile animal which appeared to possess the best features of both its progenitors. Little more is known about the development of the heavy horses in the area until after the First Crusade, when Robert, Count of Rotrou, bought back Arab stallions and, once again, these were crossed with the heavy horses. Then, in 1760, the Royal Stud at Le Pin made Arab stallions available to local breeders. These three major infusions of oriental blood were highly successful, and some of the Arab characteristics have, as described, been retained to the present day; although it is, perhaps, a little Gallic exaggeration to say that the horse is 'an Arab influenced by the climate and the agricultural work for which it has been used over the centuries.'

The Revolution in France was no less disastrous to the Percheron than to the other French breeds, and the suppression of the studs spelled near extinction for the handsome horse; but, by the early years of the 19th century, a recovery had been staged. A further boost to the breed's prestige was received with the introduction of two great Arab stallions, Godolphin and Gallipoly. The son of the latter, Jean le Blanc, foaled at Mauves-sur-Huisne in 1830, was to become one of the most famous Percheron stallions of all times. These later crosses with Arabs and carefully selected examples of the Percherons already in the area can be said to have laid the true foundations for the world-wide popularity of the modern breed.

The Percheron, as with other heavies, reached its zenith between 1880 and 1920 and, as will be described, was in demand in many countries – the United States, Australia, South America, South Africa and Britain. More recently, Japan has been added to the list of countries with a Percheron Breed Society.

Within its own breeding areas in France, the Percheron had developed into a number of sub-races of varieties, and by 1966, these numbered no fewer than eight. These were: those bred in the fifty cantons of the Perche area; the draught horse of Maine, bred in La Mayenne, the west of the Sarthe and north of Maine-le-Loire; the Nivernais draught horse, a very important type, usually large and with a black coat, bred in the Nievre district; the Augeron draught horse, bred in the Pay d'Auge; the Berrichon, found in the Cher and the Indre districts; the Bourbonnais, from around Allier, and which died out in 1923; the Loire

Percherons on parade at the State Stud at Haras du Pin in Normandy.

draught horse, for which a stud book was started in 1933 and finally, the draught horse of Saône-et-Loire.

There was considerable discussion about the wisdom of continuing to recognise all these varieties, and in 1966, the Percheron Horse Society decided to admit to its stud book (started in 1883) the horses from Maine, Augeron, the Berrichon and the Nivernais – thus bringing together all the most important varieties of the breed.

At the present time, the breed in France has just two types – the Grand Taille and the Petite Taille – the large and the small height, also known as the Gros Trait and the Postier. The Grand Taille are the largest animals, standing up to 16.3 hands (170.2 cm.) and weighing about 2,200 lb. (1,000 kg.). The Postier stand up to about 16.1 hands (165 cm.) and weigh up to 1,980 lb. (900 kg.). The Postier is rather more elegant, and with much more active paces, although it must be said that the Grand Taille moves with remarkable agility for such a large horse.

While the Percheron has continued to flourish in France and is now, alas, bred so very much for the meat market, it has since the middle of the last century become firmly established in many other countries, and its use and development in these are of great interest.

The Percheron is said to be the first heavy horse taken out to Australia in the days of the early settlements. The actual dates are a little uncertain, but it could even have been the beginning of the 19th century. The chapter on the Australian Draught Horse has given some idea of the vital part played by the heavy horses in the early days, and it is certain that Percherons were very much involved in these pioneering times.

More detailed information is available from 1913, when a stallion and two mares, Larigot, Lesion and Lanouille, were imported by the Kadlunga Stud in South Australia, and subsequently stallions (some bearing famous prefixes) were imported from France, England and Canada. The nucleus of breeding stock was maintained by Kadlunga, and later by the Agricultural Department of New South Wales, and the Foxlow and Newstead Studs, also in New South Wales.

In 1976, the Newstead Stud was dispersed, and a number of purchasers at the dispersal sale formed the Percheron Horse Breeders' Association. With less than fifty pure-bred females registered in Australia, members of the Association realised that new blood was needed. In 1978, Hales Argo and Hales Chiron were imported from England

and in the same year, Hermes, bred in France, was imported (the first French-bred Percheron to arrive in Australia for nearly forty years) by Mr and Mrs Park, of the Kamilaroi Stud in Queensland. Since his arrival one of Hermes's colts has been exported to New Zealand; this was another 'first' – the first Percheron imported into that country since 1939.

Since 1978, more stock has been introduced, and Association members are pursuing both a 'grading up' programme, and an out-crossing programme to produce a variety of very useful cross-breds. One of the most interesting programmes of up-grading (started long before the Association was formed, in fact) was undertaken for an important practical purpose by the Commonwealth Serum Laboratories. They bought two imported stallions in 1958, and over the years they have graded up a large number of horses, using further pure-bred blood from the Kadlunga and Newstead studs. The horses are used in what is known as the 'bleeding' programme, for the production of anti-venene for the treatment of snake and spider bites (both significant hazards in Australian country life) and for vaccines and serums.

In South Australia, the Mounted Police have a tradition of riding grey horses, and have undertaken a breeding programme to produce a half-bred Percheron mare to supply future generations of greys for the Force, while in Victoria the police have a half-bred presented by the Commonwealth Serum Laboratories.

Percheron stallions have been sold to Northern Australia, where they are used in cross-breeding to produce strong, active stock horses, capable of great endurance over the long distances and in the extreme heat of that vast country. The uses are typical of the great cattle country of the Northern Territory, where the heavier part-breds are employed as cattle horses to rope unbranded cattle and 'snig', them to a ramp where they are held for branding; they are also used when cattle are being handled on an open 'camp' where there is no crush or corral. Also in the north of Australia, one breeder has, for the last eighteen years or so, been cross-breeding Percherons with Arabs, and has standardised a definite type, approximately one-quarter Percheron, which withstands the demanding conditions of the work of a cattle station extremely well.

Not all cross-breeding, however, is for work. A number of Percherons are being crossed to produce top-class competition horses for show jumping, dressage, hunting and harness classes.

Pulling competitions are really 'catching on' in Australia, since the first major one was held at Taree Show in New South Wales in 1979. Percherons, with their enormous draught power, have dominated these contests, and an unofficial world record is thought to have been set up by a pure-bred mare who pulled 3,410 lb. (1,545 kg.) over the prescribed 15 ft. (4.5 m.). This was 2.84 times her own weight. In 1980 a pure-bred gelding pulled the same weight, which was 2.77 times his own weight, to win the national championship. Pulling horses in Australia, as elsewhere, are carefully trained for the events. Those belonging to Mr and Mrs Park, at Kamiloroi Stud, train daily for two

A Percheron showing his paces at the State Stud – a good example of controlled power.

or three months, using timber and gradually increasing the weight.

An interesting side-light on Percherons around the world, and the extremes of climate in which they work, is provided by a breeder in the Falkland Islands who is a member of the Australian Percheron Horse Breeders' Association. In the Falklands they cross the Percherons with local stock, principally the Criolla, to produce stock horses which stand the rugged conditions better than any other breed.

The country, however, to which the greatest number of Percherons were exported is undoubtedly the United States. Whether the breed reached America or Australia first is a moot point, but the first Percherons arrived in the USA in 1839, sent by Edward Harris, of New Jersey, when he was travelling in France. In 1851, Dr Marcus Brown, of Circleville, Ohio, imported two grey stallions and by 1870, the trade was well-established. Rather remarkably, the first American stud book was produced in 1876 – some seven years prior to the first stud book in the breed's homeland. Admittedly it was entitled the 'Norman' stud book, but the name was amended to Percheron soon afterwards. The stud book was the outcome of a meeting of ten men – owners and breeders – in Chicago in 1876, with the subsequent formation of The National Association of Importers and Breeders of Norman Horses. The name was changed to 'Percheron-Norman' in 1878, then to The Percheron Horse Society of America, and finally The Percheron Horse Association of America, which was founded in 1905, in succession to the older societies which had been disbanded.

The ten years from 1880 was a time of remarkable expansion in the breed in America, and the establishment of some of its most famous blood lines. Two stallions, Brilliant 1899, and his son, Brilliant, both living during that decade, could well be regarded as the most influential stallions in the breed's history in the United States. The market for Percherons was astonishing, with prices as high as $5,000 being paid for single animals. The popularity of the breed was enormous and was, to a large extent, killing the market for the English Shires – and for one important reason. The Americans preferred the clean legs of the Percheron to the hairy legs of the Shire.

It was said that in the 1880s, some 5,000 stallions were exported to America, and about half that number of mares. In the 1890s, however, depression hit the States, and this had a profound effect, both good and bad, on the Percheron breeding industry. Imports were drastically curtailed, which led to more reliance being placed on American breeding stock. In spite of this, many of the important studs were dispersed, and a number of good animals lost in the process; but, on the credit side, top quality horses became more widely spread through the country. Times improved, and the breed began to recover, with surprising rapidity. In 1900, there were 1,634 Percheron breeders, but by 1910, this had increased to 5,338. Registrations of horses jumped from 1,490 in the decade 1890 to 1900, to 31,900 between 1900 and 1910.

The American Percheron Horse Society saw in this period what they considered to be the nearly perfect draught horse, the stallion Calypso being chosen as the all-time ideal type. Unbelievable sums were paid for top horses – one called Carnot sold for $40,000 – a staggering

Horses, many heavies among them, shared the horror and desolation of the First World War with the soldiers, as reflected in this scene in France (left). They too were issued gas-masks (above) and when injured some were lucky enough to be taken to special Veterinary Hospitals like No. 5 (top) at Abbeville, France. This photograph, showing the horses lined up outside the hospital, was taken in April 1918.

amount of money in those days, and unlikely to be topped even at today's inflated prices.

The Americans have always liked large horses, and some of the biggest and tallest on record have been bred in that country. One such features in the *Guinness Book of Records*. This was the Percheron Dr Le Gear, foaled in 1902, who grew to an immense 21 hands (213.4 cm.) – 7 ft. at the withers! – and weighed just under 27 cwt. (1,370 kg.).

Britain was very late on the Percheron scene, but the breed made up for lost time with unusual rapidity, and the British version is now firmly established with the Suffolk, the Shire and the Clydesdale as one of the four draught breeds of the country. It was in its role of war horse that the Percheron first came to the notice of the British; not, as in Europe, as a charger in a great medieval battle, but as a draught horse in the terrible conditions of France during the First World War.

There was a huge demand for horses in that conflict, for pulling the guns and supply wagons; a study of the conditions and the horses in France convinced the Army Remount authorities that Percherons were ideal – strong, willing, and so docile that they could be handled easily, even by soldiers who were, in some instances, unaccustomed to dealing with horses.

In the retreat from Mons, and in the battles of the Marne and Ypres in 1914, the British Army lost 12 per cent of its horses. Had losses on that scale continued throughout the year, 30 per cent of the total would have been killed. Clearly, something had to be done, and by 1915 something *was* being done. Thousands of horses, mostly of Percheron type or Percheron cross-breds, were being imported from the United States and Canada. The British Remount Commission had the unenviable task of arranging shipment from North America, and this was fraught with difficulties. First of all, the horses had to be treated against glanders (a highly contagious disease of the lymphatic system), then sent by train to the embarkation ports. The Americans, mercifully for the horses, would not allow them to travel for more than thirty-six hours at a time, so stopping points had to be arranged. During the journey, and in spite of precautions, nearly three-quarters of them contracted a type of influenza known as 'shipping fever', which sometimes developed into pneumonia – and as it did not necessarily develop immediately the horses had to be kept at the embarkation ports for up to seven weeks before being loaded for the Atlantic crossing.

At the best of times the shipment of horses is probably as unpleasant for them as it is for those who look after them. After being crowded into small stalls below decks, often with insufficient head-room, always without room for exercise, the horses when they arrived in Britain had to undergo a recovery period before they were shipped across to France – well, the figures tell their own shocking story. Five hundred thousand British Army horses died during or as a result of the war – and many of these were of Percheron type.

Many of the horses were the progeny of Percherons put to light American mares, and they came in three sizes. Light artillery horses were short-legged, short-backed and very strong, standing from 15.2 to 16 hands (157.5 to 162.6 cm.) and weighing about 1,200 lb. (550 kg.); while the other two heavy artillery horses weighed about 1,400 and 1,500 lb. (650 and 680 kg.), with the heavier ones being three-quarter-bred Percheron, and the smaller, Shire type. The gallant, willing, amenable Percheron endeared itself to the British soldier, and laid the foundations for the breed's subsequent introduction and popularity in Britain after the war.

In the meantime, at home in England, the war looked as if it could go on for years, and the authorities were faced with the ever-increasing demand for more horses for France. The ability of the Percheron stallions to produce good, sound stock from a wide variety of (often indifferent) mares had not gone unnoticed, and it was decided to start a breeding programme in Britain. Lord Lonsdale and a well-known breeder, Mr Henry Overman, went to France and bought between them two stallions (the four-year-old Misanthrope, a beautiful animal and a great mover, and the three-year-old Nonius), and twelve mares. The following year, thirty-three mares and twelve stallions were brought over, and by January 1918, a group of enthusiastic breeders had founded the Percheron Society under the presidency of Lord Lonsdale.

Above A black Percheron stallion. This colour is particularly popular in North America.

Opposite Harnessed together in line abreast, the Percherons are a splendid sight at their 100th Annual Show at Haras du Pin in Normandy.

Shire breeders were understandably appalled by all this, and as Keith Chivers wrote in *The Shire Horse* their comments were forthright if inelegant: 'While we're fighting the damned Hun, they're going to bring in a b*** French horse.' What was worse, it was the same horse that had, to all intents and purposes, caused the demise of the American export trade in Shires!

But the Percherons had arrived, and the Breed Society expanded rapidly. Owners queued to obtain nominations for their mares to the available stallions. The horses proved ideal agricultural animals, and the farmers liked their clean legs and economic feeding. They liked, too, their delightfully docile and amenable temperament – a few hours was all that it took to break the average Percheron to farm gears. Percherons and their crosses were used in horse buses in London and in other cities throughout Britain – one estimate suggested that 90 per cent of London's horse buses were pulled by cross-bred Percherons.

The breed in Britain established itself in the heart of heavy-horse country – in Cambridgeshire (the breed offices have been in Cambridge for many years), Norfolk and Lincolnshire, as well as further north in Durham.

The British Percheron Horse Society produced its own breed standards, which require that it should be a heavy draught horse possessing great muscular development, combined with style and activity. It should possess ample bone of good quality, and give a general impression of balance and power. The colour is grey or black, with a minimum of white. No other colour in stallions is eligible for entry in the stud book. Skin and coat should be of fine quality. Stallions should not be less than 16.3 hands (170.2 cm.) and mares not less than 16.1 hands (165 cm.) but width and depth must not be sacrificed to height, at maturity. Stallions should weigh between 18 and 20 cwt. (913 and 1,015 kg.), and mares from 16 to 18 cwt. (812 to 913 kg.).

The head is wide across the eyes, which should be full and docile; the ears are medium in size and erect; the cheek is deep, curved on the lower side, and not long from eye to nose. The horse should have an intelligent expression. The ideal neck should be strong and not short, and in the case of stallions should bear a fully arched crest. The chest should be wide, and the shoulders deep and well-laid. A strong, short back is required; the ribs should be wide and deep, and deep at the flanks. The hindquarters must be of exceptional width and long from hips to tail, avoiding any suggestion of a goose rump. The limbs are, of course, all important, and should show strong arms and full second thighs, with big knees and broad hocks. There should be heavy, flat bone, with short cannons, and pasterns of medium length. The feet should be of reasonable size, of good quality hard blue horn. The limbs should be as clean and free from hair as possible. The action must be typical of the breed, straight, bold, and with a long free stride, rather than short, snappy action. The hocks must be well flexed and kept close.

The British Society holds an annual breed show, with classes for in-hand breeding, and harness animals.

Right *A good type of Percheron exhibited at the Royal Show at Stoneleigh in Warwickshire. Note the lack of feathering on the legs, and the typical dappling of the coat.*

Opposite *Showing Percherons in France. The use of two handlers is quite general in Europe.*

The French Society also holds an annual show and in 1982, the 100th was held at the French national stud at Haras du Pin in Normandy. It was a great event, set in a beautiful valley overlooked by the elegant buildings of the stud. Over 150 animals competed in a widely ranging programme of classes and demonstrations. The breeding classes included those for stallions of various ages and of both sizes, and similar classes were held for youngstock, and for mares with and without foals.

Showing in France (and indeed in much of Europe) differs from that in Britain, Australia and America. The in-hand classes are judged, not by a single judge, but by a jury of three, and the exhibits are shown by two handlers. The jury stands in front of or in a tent at one end of the arena, and the horses are brought in singly. Each is led by one handler, and accompanied by another who carries a lunging whip, and both are usually turned out neatly in white shirts and trousers (the latter often with coloured stripes down the side-seams) and white running shoes. The horse is then 'stood up' in front of the judges, with one handler flicking the whip to keep it alert. Next, the horse is walked and then trotted away from and back towards the judges. The handler with the whip follows behind and occasionally gives the animal a bit of 'encouragement' to move more actively. When the judges have finished their assessment the horse is led out, and the next brought in – and so on through the class. When all have been judged individually, a selected number are then called into the ring for final appraisal. While still parading their horses, the exhibitors are handed metal enamelled plaques, instead of the more customary (to British exhibitors, at least) rosettes. Until the result is announced, it is far from easy to tell which horse has actually won the class.

At the 100th show, judging of the breeding classes occupied the morning. After lunch, demonstrations were staged. These included ploughing with teams of three or four horses, while other animals worked in harness, drawing historic vehicles, or farm wagons piled high with straw. There was an enthralling braiding competition, in which the French experts demonstrated their skill at plaiting manes and tails.

Most spectacular of all was the grand finale, when groups of horses were shown in hand. Mares, stallions and foals took part, harnessed together in line abreast, with a handler at each side – as can be seen on page 76. The groups were lined up and judged while stationary, and then they set off round the arena, first at the walk, and then at the trot. And what a sight it was – some of the groups contained as many as eight horses – as they thundered around, preceded and followed by running handlers cracking their whips. It says so much for the marvellous temperament of the Percheron that all the animals – from the smallest and youngest foal, to the biggest stallions – took the whole display in their stride, and trotted actively yet sensibly round the ring, a wonderful picture of controlled power.

The Rhenish-German Heavy

The Rhenish-German horse, although now one of the rarest of all the heavy breeds, is nonetheless of great importance, as it is regarded as the nucleus of the other German heavies. A few are kept at the State Stud at Warendorf, and there are less than a dozen private breeders who between them own just two stallions and fifteen registered brood mares – a frighteningly small representation of what was once the most numerous breed in Germany. The tragic decline can be judged from the fact that before the Second World War the breed accounted for 80 per cent of all heavy horses in Germany, and even as comparatively recently as 1949 there were more than 26,000 Rhenish-Germans.

The breed has a relatively short history, having been developed only in the last quarter of the 19th century – the culmination of a breeding programme begun about 1839, and aimed at producing a useful agricultural and draught animal. Much of the breeding was carried out at the Wickrath State Stud and on private studs in the Rhineland. Initially, a great mixture of breeds was used, including the three British breeds – Clydesdale, Suffolk, and Shire – as well as the French Percheron and Boulonnais, and the Danish Jutland. For some considerable time the results, in terms of conformation and performance, were not very successful, but in the 1870s the introduction of Belgian Heavy and Belgian Ardennes blood began to produce a strong, well-built, short-legged animal that had good bone and free movement, and was economical to keep.

From about 1880 this kind of breeding programme began to be followed by studs in most of the German breeding areas – the Rhine, Lower Saxony, East Prussia, Westphalia and Hessen – and from then until the First World War breeding flourished; this period could be called the 'boom time' of the German heavy horse.

As so often happens when breeding is practised in different areas using a variety of bloods, variation of types emerged, and these in time were given different names, although their genetic background was very similar. (Anyone familiar with the modern German riding horse breeds will recognise the parallel situation – the breeds

Left   A Westphalian striding out vigorously.

Opposite   Westphalian Heavy Draught stallions in the famous parade at the stallion station, Warendorf in Germany. The Westphalian is a breed that has been influenced by Rhenish-German blood.

bear different names but are not markedly dissimilar in type or appearance.) In the Rhineland and in Westphalia a heavy type was bred, while in other regions medium to lightweight animals were needed.

The most important strain, however, known initially as the Rhenish-Belgian (thus emphasising the Belgian contribution to its development), was based on Wickrath and the surrounding districts and in 1892, the first stud book was published. In 1917 the breed name was changed to Rhenish-German, in an effort to promote the home-bred animals, but Belgian blood continued to be used for some time. The Wickrath Stud remained as the principal breeding centre until after the Second World War, but it was closed in 1957, and the stallions sent to Warendorf. In 1973, those stallions remaining at Warendorf were dispersed among private breeders.

The modern Rhenish-German is a powerful, stocky animal of handsome appearance, standing about 16.2 hands (167.6 cm.) and weighing in the region of a ton. The head, although inclined to be a little heavy in some animals, is noted for its very kind eye – an indication of its docile and amenable temperament. The neck is short and strong, and bears a thick, often double-sided mane. The chest is deep and wide, endowing the horse with good pulling power, and the shoulders are suitably sloped for the type of draught work undertaken. The back is short and strong, the body shows great depth, and the hindquarters, while sloping, are heavily muscled and strong in appearance. The limbs are markedly short and strong, and bear a moderate amount of feathering. The breed is noted for its good, sound feet. The most usual colours are chestnut (often with flaxen mane and tail) and roan. The overall picture is one of strength and energy, and the Rhenish-German horse in its heyday was renowned as a willing worker. It seems so sad that the breed, having been of such importance in its homeland, should now appear to be on the verge of extinction, after an effective life of less than a century.

One of the breeds that has been influenced to some extent (at least in post-Second-World-War days) by the Rhenish-German, is the Westphalian Heavy Horse. The breed was based on the importation in 1881 of the Belgian Ardennes stallions, Flick and Flock, who stood in the Ruhr region, where the demand for heavy horses in the steel and coal industries was widespread. In 1904 the State Stud at Warendorf published the first Westphalian Stud Book, and by 1939 there were approximately 20,000 of the breed within the 'home' region. There are now less than twenty stallions and about 150 mares remaining. Five of the stallions are used in parades at Warendorf, and occasionally cover a few mares, while there are about ten in private ownership.

The Hessen Heavy Horse was developed during the last twenty years of the 19th century at the State Stud at Darmstadt and at Dillenburg, using Belgian and, later, Rhenish-German bloodlines. The breed was recognised in the early 20th century. At the time of writing there are just five licensed stallions, including the Rhenish-German Nippes II, and the Hessen-bred Ziether, with his sons Zigeuner and Zamborius. There are less than twenty brood mares in private hands. The breed is used (obviously in small numbers) for lumber work in the Hessen region transporting timber from the forests.

The Russian Heavy Breeds

Heavy horses are present in the Soviet Union in large numbers. Some are widely used in agriculture, while others are bred for meat. Of the best known breeds – the Russian Heavy Draught, the Soviet Heavy Draught, the Lithuanian Heavy Harness Horse, and the Vladimir Heavy Draught – a staggering 531,000 animals (of which 34,000 were purebred) were registered in 1970. By 1974 this figure had dropped by some tens of thousands, and no doubt has continued to do so, but it is still a very great number of working horses.

The oldest of the breeds, the Russian Heavy Draught, was established about a century ago, but the others are of more recent origin. The Russian Heavy Draught is also the smallest of the four breeds, with stallions averaging about 14.3 hands (149.9 cm.) and weighing about 1,302 lb. (590 kg.). Their average girth is 6 ft. 6 in., and they have about 8.7 in. (22 cm.) of bone. The mares stand about 14.2 hands (148 cm.), weight 1,236 lb. (560 kg.) with a girth of 6 ft. 3 in. (188 cm.) and 8.3 in. (20–21 cm.) of bone.

It is an attractive little horse with a lively, yet calm temperament, exceptionally free movement, and a strong constitution that makes it economical to keep. As will be seen, it does have some weaknesses in conformation. The head, however, is light, 'dry', and with a wide forehead and bright, friendly eyes. The neck is excellent, quite long, muscular and very elegantly curved, with a handsome crest in the case of stallions. The withers are broad, not very well defined, and lead to a broad back that is rather too long, and consequently not particularly strong. The loins are straight, wide, and muscular, the croup is wide, and the tail reasonably well-set. Both mane and tail are long and profuse. The legs are short and strong, with a little short feathering, but the hind legs are often sickle-hocked. The ribs are well-sprung, and the body barrel-shaped. The most usual colours are chestnut and strawberry roan, with the occasional bay or bay-roan.

The Russian Heavy Draught is ideally suited in height and weight to the draught work which is so much a part of agriculture. In working capacity tests the breed performs extremely well, and, considering its small size, compares favourably with the other heavy breeds.

The following records have been set by the breed in performance tests, and it is interesting to compare these figures with those of the larger, heavier breeds described later in this chapter.

The stallion Stil covered a distance of 2 km. at the walk in 15 minutes 22 seconds with a tractive power of 150 kg.; the mare Geraldika trotted a distance of 2 km. in 5 min. 21 sec. with a tractive power of 50 kg.; the mare Palatka covered 1,091 metres with a tractive power of 300 kg., and the stallion Raskat recorded a maximum tractive capacity of 779 kg. On a less formal occasion, it was reported that a team of three Russian Heavy Draughts pulled a vehicle laden with 70 people, and the stallion Satyr pulled a record load of fifteen tons. Thus, all in all, the breed's rather weak back and sickle-hocked legs do not appear to be a very great disadvantage.

In addition to being economical feeders, the Russian Heavy Draught horses mature quickly – at eighteen months they have reached 96 to 97 per cent of their adult height and 75 per cent of the adult weight, and they are fully grown as three year olds. They live to a great age, and have the added advantage of a good fertility rate, averaging 80 to 85 per cent, but sometimes reaching 95 per cent. Many mares are still breeding in their middle and late twenties.

The breed is used widely in the north and north-west of the Soviet Union, in the Urals, the Ukraine, the Caucasus, Siberia, and Belorussia. The best representatives are found on the Kuedin Stud near Perm, the Novoaleksandrivsk Stud near Voroshilograd, and the Krasnoarmeisk Stud near Sverdlovak.

The Russian Draught was officially registered with the Ministry of Agriculture in 1952, and was originally based on small Belgian Ardennes stallions that were imported about 100 years ago. Although chosen for their valuable qualities of good movement, strong constitution, and economic feeding requirements, the Ardennes had some conformational weaknesses. Through selective breeding most of these were eliminated so successfully that at the Paris Exhibition in 1900 a stallion from the Khrenov Stud won the coveted Gold Medal. In the Soviet Union the breed became very popular indeed, and was bred at 376 studs, including the state studs at Khrenov and Derkul, and on private studs.

Tragically, few of the breed survived the Revolution, but from those that did, stock was bred that eventually produced a medium-sized agricultural horse which was then given the name of Russian Heavy Draught. Today, line breeding is practised extensively, but a limited amount of new blood is introduced from time to time by crossing with the related Soviet Heavy Draught. It is interesting that the breeding stock on the studs is used for agricultural work, thus operating a form of selection for endurance, working ability and good movement.

In 1974, there were 170,000 registered Russian Heavy Draught Horses, only a small proportion of which were purebred.

From the smallest Russian breed to the largest – the strong and bulky Vladimir Heavy Draught. The stallions stand, on average, 16.1 hands (165 cm.), weigh 1,668 lb. (758 kg.), have a girth of 6 ft. 9 in. (207 cm.), and $9\frac{3}{4}$ in. (24.6 cm.) of bone. Mares stand about 15.3 hands (160 cm.), weigh 1,507 lb. (685 kg.), have a girth of 6 ft. 5 in. (196 cm.), and $9\frac{1}{4}$ in. (23 cm.) of bone.

The Lithuanian Heavy Harness was developed by crossing Swedish Ardennes with local Zhmud riding horses.

The breed was evolved at studs in the Ivanov and Vladimir areas east of Moscow, using Shires, and particularly Clydesdales on local mares. The most influential Clydesdale stallions were Lord James and Border Brand, imported in 1910, and Glen Albin, imported in 1923. The mares are said to have contributed significantly to the breed's qualities of endurance and adaptability. It was not, however, recognised as an individual breed until 1946. The most widely used system of breeding Vladimirs today is inbreeding to outstanding foundation stallions, and to crosses of lines that blend well. It is a very early maturing breed, with three year olds being introduced to stud duties and to draught work. A fertility rate of 75 per cent to 80 per cent is normal.

A feature of the Vladimir Heavy Draught is its very free and energetic action, and individuals are often used for pulling the famous Russian troikas, as well as the more usual agricultural vehicles and implements. The breed does well in weight-pulling trials. The stallion Gomon covered a distance of 2 km. at walk in 13 minutes 4 seconds with a tractive power of 150 kg.; the mare Grozny established an absolute all-breeds record at the trot by covering a distance of 2 km. in 4 minutes 34 seconds with a tractive power of 50 kg.; the mare Kartinka covered 834 m. with a tractive power of 300 kg. and the stallion Ekar set a record of pulling with 820 kg.

Left Russian Heavy Draught. The oldest and the smallest of the four principal heavy breeds found in the Soviet Union. They are based on Belgian Ardennes and there are well over 100,000 registered in the Stud book. Chestnut is one of the most common colours in the breed.

Below The fine head of a Russian Heavy Draught Horse.

Opposite The Vladimir Heavy Draught, recognised as a breed in 1946. Two Clydesdale stallions, Lord James and Border Brand, were influential in the development of the Vladimir breed.

In appearance, the Valdimir is perhaps less attractive than the Russian Heavy, as it has a large, rather long head with a pronounced Roman nose, in contrast to the more quality head of its smaller countryman. The neck is long and muscular, the withers well-defined and, as in the Russian, the back is broad, but rather long and lacking in strength. The croup is long, broad, and sloping. The chest is deep, but the body is rather flat-ribbed, which is not a good feature in a draught horse. The legs are long, and some specimens of the breed have thick feathering, and show a tendency to cracked heels. The predominant colour of the Vladimir is rich bay, with a few blacks and chestnuts which have white markings on the head and legs. The breed is noted for its good temperament.

Possibly the most widely used heavy in the country is the Soviet Heavy Draught, which is said to be the best adapted to the severe climatic conditions. It is bred in all the agricultural regions, both in European Russia and in the Central Asian Republic. The best studs are in the Vladimir, Gorky, Tambov and Yaroslav provinces, in the Ukraine and in the Mordovian Autonomous Republic.

The breed was formed by using Belgian stallions, imported in the second half of the 19th century, on local cross-bred mares of harness type, who in turn were derived from Ardennes, Percherons and the indigenous Bityugs. Particularly in the north-east of Russia, the studs produced large number of pedigree animals of heavy draught type which differed markedly from the Belgians. They were described as 'drier', better proportioned, more mobile, and in general, rather smaller than the Belgians, and were first registered as a separate breed in 1952.

There are now several established blood lines within the breed which produce some variation of type. On the male side there are eight lines, of which the most influential was founded by the stallion Bozhe, and carried on by his two sons, Rezhim and Rumb, in the middle of the 1930s. They have imparted a lighter build, and better conformation which some of the other lines lack. It is through this line that some early Suffolk blood had most influence, giving more freedom of action and refinement of appearance which is lacking in, for instance, the Zhasmin line, which is rather coarse and less active. Coarseness, but with good qualities of endurance, are features of the Fleitist line. This line also has notably weak backs and very steeply sloping croups.

Only one female line is regarded as being of great significance, and that is the Kleron-Remi. The mares of this line, when mated with stallions of the Boxhe or the Zhasmin line, produce excellent stock, of good conformation, size, and strength. They are good workers.

The Soviet Heavy Draught has a medium-sized head, with a very muscular neck of short to medium length. The withers are low and wide, the back broad and sometimes weak. The loins are straight and wide, and the croup has a pronounced slope. The chest is wide and the ribs well-sprung. The legs (which carry some feathering) are not the breed's best point, often showing weak fetlocks, pigeon toes, weak pasterns and sickle hocks. The foot, however, is usually well-shaped. Individual animals incline to fleshiness. The principal colours are chestnut and strawberry roan, with occasional bays and bay-roans.

The average height of a stallion is between 15.3 and 16 hands (161 cm.), the girth nearly 7 ft. (211 cm.) and there is usually 9.8 in. (25 cm.) of bone. The mares stand between 15.1 and 15.2 hands (15.5 cm.), with a girth of 6 ft. 5 in. (196.2 cm.) and about $9\frac{1}{2}$ in. (23.9 cm.) of bone. Stallions average about 1,722 lb. (780 kg.), and mares 1,443 lb. (654 kg.).

The breed matures early, with young stock being used for agriculture from the age of two and a half years, and they take up stud duties from the age of three. At six months colt foals may weigh between 806 and 827 lb. (365 and 375 kg.), and as a yearling may tip the scales at 1,159–1,192 lb. (525–540 kg.). The breed has a relatively low fertility rate of between 65 per cent and 75 per cent with the mares continuing to breed until their seventeenth and eighteenth year.

The Soviet Heavy Draught's less than perfect conformation has evidently not affected its great qualities of strength and endurance, with individual animals setting up records in weight pulling and endurance tests. The absolute weight-pulling record was set up by a six-year-old

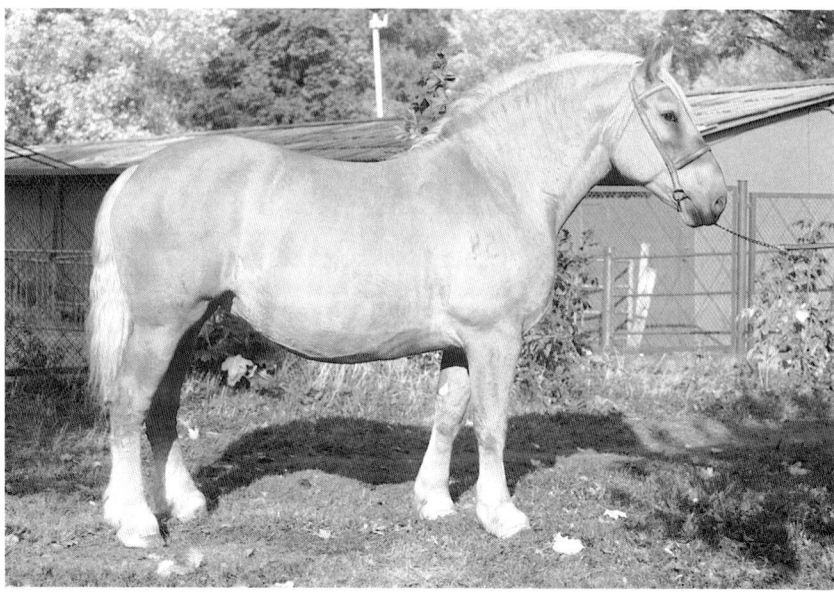

Above Vladimir Heavy Draught – the largest of the four principal Russian breeds.

Opposite The Soviet Heavy Draught. A six-year-old Soviet stallion set up a national absolute weight-pulling record when he moved a load of 22,990 kg. (nearly 23 tons) over a distance of 35 km.

stallion who moved a load weighing 22,990 kg. (50,750 lb. – nearly 23 tons) over a distance of 35 km. In 1971 the stallion Zubr covered 2 km. at the walk in 11 minutes 52 seconds, with a tractive power of 150 kg., and in 1968, the mare Rafiya trotted 2 km. in 4 minutes 53 seconds with a tractive power of 50 kg. The mare Zherd set an endurance record, covering a distance of 1,138 km. with a tractive power of 300 kg., while in 1968 the mare Zavod produced a maximum tractive power of 851 kg.

The last of the Russian breeds to be discussed is the Lithuanian Heavy Harness Horse which, as its name suggests, has its origins in the Lithuanian region of the Soviet Union. As far back as the 1880s, a breeding society for Zhmud horses was formed in the region. They were small riding-type horses, and when the need for heavy agricultural horses arose, they were crossed with various heavy breeds, notably with Swedish Ardennes. Just under 600 Swedish Ardennes were imported, including 175 stallions. They were selected for type and conformation which would, it was thought, when allied with the hardiness of the Zhmud, produce a strong, amenable agricultural horse.

Crosses were made, and after continued selective breeding, much of which has been carried out since the Revolution in the state studs at Zhagar, Neman, Vilnius and Sudav, the breed was finally recognised in 1963, and now has its own stud book. As well as in Lithuania, the breed is found all over north-west Russia, and in Kazakhstan, where the Lithuanians are crossed with local mares to produce animals for the meat market.

The overall impression of the Lithuanian horse is of a very strong, muscular, but not notably good-looking horse. It has a fairly large head, a short, muscular neck, and wide withers of average height and length. The back is broad and straight, but sometimes dipping behind the withers. The loins are wide and strong, the croup broad with a pronounced slope, and the rib-cage barrel-shaped and very well-developed. The legs are strong and squarely set. The predominant colour of the breed is chestnut, but bays, bay-roans and chestnuts are also found.

The breed is noted for its strong constitution and placid temperament. It is long-lived, and both mares and stallions are used at stud up to the age of about twenty years.

Individual animals have performed well in weight-pulling trials, particularly at the walk, which is the breed's best pace. The stallion Aras covered a distance of 2 km. at walk in 13 minutes 20 seconds with a tractive power of 150 kg.; the mare Vilnis covered a distance of 2 km. at trot in 5 minutes 1 second with a tractive power of 50 kg.; the stallion Gintaras covered 1,397 m. with a tractive power of 300 kg. and the stallion Trimitas recorded a maximum weight-pulling capacity of 860 kg.

The average height of a stallion is 15.2 hands (157.5 cm.), with a girth of 7 ft. 4 in. (197 cm.) and $9\frac{1}{2}$ in. (24 cm.) of bone. The mares stand about 15.1 hands (155 cm.), with a girth of 6 ft. 6 in. (192 cm.) and 9 in. (23 cm.) of bone. Stallions weigh on average 1,545 lb. (700 kg.) and mares 1,424 lb. (645 kg.).

The Russian Heavy Draught See THE RUSSIAN HEAVY BREEDS.

Lithuanian Heavy Draught, widely used for agriculture in the Soviet Union, was recognised as recently as 1963.

The Schleswig-Holstein Heavy

The Schleswig-Holstein (commonly known as the Schleswiger) is the smaller of the two best-known German breeds, standing only about 15.2 to 16 hands (157.5 to 162.6 cm.) to the Rhenish-German's 16.2 hands (167.6 cm.) and weighing, on average, 1,766 lb. (800 kg.). As with the Rhenish-German, the numbers of this attractive breed are small, but active steps are now, thankfully, being taken to preserve and increase them.

The breed has had a somewhat chequered history, due in large part to the fact that the province of Schleswig has passed from Danish to German sovereignty and back on more than one occasion. The Schleswiger had its origins around 1866, when the province became a part of Germany; but while it was still part of Denmark, the heavy horses in the area were influenced by the English stallion Oppenheim, which played so important a role in the development of the Jutland breed. Indeed, there is a resemblance between the Jutland and the Schleswiger to this day – dating no doubt from this early influence. During the closing years of the last century, a variety of lighter blood was introduced, including Cleveland Bay, Thoroughbred, Yorkshire Coach Horse and the Danish Fredericksborg – but there is little or no sign of the influence of those breeds in today's horses. In 1891 the Society of Schleswiger Breeders was founded.

The Schleswiger declined in numbers and in quality when the province returned to Danish ownership during the First World War, but with its ultimate reversion to Germany, there were thoughts of merging the remaining animals with the Rhenish-German breed. This was not done, however, and the Schleswiger not only survived but came to occupy a leading position among the German heavies. The survival of the breed was due to a large extent to the introduction of outside blood in the shape of the grey Boulonnais stallion, Faust, and the excellent Breton stallion, Hasta Breton.

The breed really reached its peak in the years following the end of the Second World War, up until about 1950. The Society of Schleswiger Breeders had a membership of 15,000, with more than 20,000 mares registered in the stud books. Although some stallions belonged to the provincial stud, the majority were privately owned. The breed was used extensively as farm working horses, in transport, forestry and, to a certain extent, by the army.

Mechanisation, however, played its customary devastating role. By the beginning of the 1970s, the number of mares had fallen to below 100 and the stallion numbers had also dropped dramatically. Nevertheless the dedicated breeders did not give up, and efforts were made to revive and improve the breed with further introductions of Breton and

Right A quartet of Schleswig-Holstein horses, the smaller of the two best known German heavy horses, standing up to 16 hands.

Opposite A charming period picture of pre-war brewery horses in Schleswig-Holstein.

A delightful study of Schleswig-Holstein mare and foal. Jutland mares and stallions have recently been introduced into the breed with the aim of increasing the Schleswigers' size.

Above *A pair of working brewery horses showing the typical German harness.*

Boulonnais blood. Most breeding was by this time centred around the northern Schleswig-Holstein town of Husum, where very high standards of stallion selection were in force.

In 1975, the breeding society opened its own headquarters, and in 1976 the 120 members sought a connection with the Schleswig-Holstein/Hamburg breeding society for ponies and small horses. An amalgamation took place, and a new society, known as the Horse Breed Book Schleswig-Holstein/Hamburg E.V. was formed. The breeding centre for the Schleswig is in the Segeburg area, under the direction of Jurgen Isenburg, a great authority on the breed.

In 1978, twenty-four foals and ten mares were registered in the Schleswig stud book; in 1979, thirty-nine mares were covered, while in 1980, twenty-four foals, three three year olds and seven older mares were registered. At the time of writing, a total of sixty-five mares and five stallions are registered in the book. Four years ago, two Jutland mares and several stallions were bought, with the aim of increasing the size and height of the Schleswiger – a move that will be watched with great interest by breeders.

The Shire

On 22nd March, 1978, the East of England Showground at Peterborough was filled with row upon row of magnificent Shire horses, a sight to gladden the hearts of Shire enthusiasts the world over. It was the occasion of the Shire Horse Society's Centenary Show – a Royal occasion, too, attended by the Society's Patron and President, Her Majesty the Queen, accompanied by the Duke of Edinburgh. But it was far more than that. It was a convincing assertion that just could not have been made fifteen years before, when the fortunes of the breed had sunk to their lowest ebb and it was in grave danger of actual extinction. Even less than ten years previously, a *combined* Shire and Percheron Show could muster just over 100 animals, whereas the Centenary Show had entries of nearly 200 registered Shires.

The story of the decline and revival of the Shire differs only in detail from that of the other British heavy breeds; it is a reflection of the industrial, agricultural and social change in Britain (and more particularly in England) over the last eighty years. But the Shire (together with its near relative the Clydesdale and, to a lesser extent, the Suffolk, because of its relative isolation in East Anglia) and its ancestors have been mirroring the changing face of Britain for far longer than that – for the greater part of 1,000 years.

But before embarking on the history of the Shire, let us look at the present-day horse. When a class of Shire stallions enters a show ring, the first impression is one of their great nobility and presence, with their forceful, deliberate and weighty walk enhancing the overall picture of restrained strength. The Shire has a lean, well-proportioned head with a slightly Roman nose, and a fairly long, well-created neck which is often so heavily muscled that it appears shorter than it actually is. The girth is impressive – between 6 and 8 ft. (1.8 and 2.4 m.) – and the back short and strong, leading to substantially muscled quarters and a well-set tail. Compared with those of the chunkier Suffolk or Ardennes, the legs appear longer, but they are very strong, with at least 11 in. (28 cm.) of bone in a stallion. The most striking feature of the legs is, of course, the feathering, which is fine, silky and straight, growing from just below the knees in front and the hocks behind. The modern breed has noticeably less feathering than its predecessors. The most popular colouring among modern breeders is black with white feathering, and, less commonly, grey – the latter being much in favour with some breweries. White markings on the lower part of the legs is considered correct, but any large splashes of white on the body, as seen in Clydesdales, is not acceptable on stallions, although viewed less seriously in mares. Colour has, in the 20th century, been governed to some extent by fashion; at one time bays and greys were sought after, whereas unpopular roan suggests a link with the Clydesdale.

The action of the Shire shows active use of knees and hocks, and the flexible fetlock joint should allow the underside of the hoof to be visible from behind at the walk. A good animal moves absolutely straight, and at the back the hocks must be close together, not wide so that 'you can push a wheel-barrow between them'.

Shire mares are, as in most breeds, rather smaller, standing between 16 and 17 hands (162.6 and 172.8 cm.) – compared with the stallion's 16.2 to 17.2 hands (167.6 to 178 cm.) – with a girth of between 5 and 7 ft. (1.5 and 2.1 m.). They must look more feminine and matronly, and the body must be relatively longer than that of the stallion, to allow room for carrying a foal.

This is a picture of the modern Shire based on the standards laid down by the Shire Horse Society, but it does not describe accurately the Shires of 100 years ago, still less the horse of the Middle Ages from which the breed has descended.

It is widely believed that the Shire has developed from the Great War Horse of medieval times, and in a sense this is so, as the first heavy horses imported into Britain, and the first heavy horses that were bred here, were for war. These imports were made after William the Conqueror's mounted army had defeated Harold's infantry – and mounted warfare became the order of the day. Not a great deal is known about the heavy horses that were brought in from Europe (other than the fact that they were a great many of them) until the reign of King John, when, in about 1199, he imported 100 black Flemish stallions to improve the general standard of heavy horses that had gradually emerged since the days of the Conqueror.

Further imports arrived throughout the next 100 years or more, and the numbers of War Horses (or Great Horses, as they are often called) increased, only, by some accounts, to be drastically reduced again by Edward II's disastrous defeat at Bannockburn. Probably as a result of this, both to prevent the Scots from acquiring more horses and to replenish the depleted stock in England, Edward III prohibited the export of horses to Scotland, and Richard II imposed price controls so that when Henry IV came to the throne, the supply of heavy horses was almost equal to the demand. But because of the civil disturbances rife during the following years, many breeders sold their horses abroad (mostly to France), partly to prevent them falling into opponents' hands; by the time Henry VII ascended the throne, the stock of heavy horses was once again depleted. Both Henry VII and Henry VIII passed laws to forbid exports, and Henry VIII, in particular, tried to enforce the breeding of larger animals by controlling the size of breeding stock. For instance, in 1540 he decreed that no one should put out to pasture any stallion that did not stand at least 15 hands (152.4 cm.) high – this was apparently, at

A pair of Shires in tandem competing at the Shire Centenary Show.

that time, regarded as quite a large horse. This is interesting, not because of its effectiveness (which was negligible) but because it tends to confirm that the 'Great' War Horse of medieval times was rather smaller than has previously been thought. (Measurements of horse armour in the Tower of London suggest that the Great Horses, although large by the standards of the day, were probably only about 15 to 15.2 hands (152.4 to 157.5 cm.), and of muscular, rather cobby build.)

By the end of Henry VIII's reign, the use of the 'Great' War Horse was becoming outmoded and as a result the breeding of this type of animal lacked purpose and went into a decline. It is important to remember that at this stage in British history, goods were carried by pack animals of moderate size over routes that could scarcely be described as roads, and agricultural work was still largely done by oxen. It was left to Henry VIII's redoubtable daughter, Elizabeth I, to set a new fashion that was, in effect, to change the direction of heavy-horse breeding in Britain. In 1564, Her Majesty acquired a coach. Because of the appalling state of the 'roads', considerable numbers of large, strong horses were needed to pull such a vehicle, and it is recounted how, in 1572, the Queen travelled to Warwick in the coach behind, 'six of the biggest and strongest horses available, and as a result was unable to sit down for days'!

Nonetheless, the fashion spread, encouraged by the royal patronage, and in due course not only people, but goods, were being hauled around the country in wagons drawn by draught horses. Perhaps even more significantly, at about the same time as the Queen acquired her coach, public stage wagons were introduced, and the role of the War Horse began to change to that of draught horse.

So at last we see the emergence of cart or draught horses – but we are still a considerable way from anything that could be recognised as a Shire. Heavy horses were still being imported from Europe, and the Elizabethan writer, Thomas Blundeville, mentions three specific breeds – the Almaine (or German), the Flemish and the Frisian. It is the second of these, the Flemish (or Flanders), that occurs again and again in the subsequent history of what was to become the Shire Horse, and this predominantly black horse from the Low Countries must be regarded as the true ancestor of the breed. The Frisian (which was, and is, always black) also played a part, but the German contribution is less easy to see.

Blundeville describes in some detail the Flemish horse, mentioning that because of its native habitat in marshland it was large, heavy and somewhat gross – features that were modified when it was bred in England to a 'finer limmed, cleaner made, and therewith light and more nimble' horse than in its native land. It is worth noting that in later years, when heavy horses were bred in the Fens in land not dissimilar to Flanders, the same type of horse emerged. Blundeville also described the contemporary English cart horse in terms that were not wholly compli-

Above Not a theme from the past, but a pair of present-day Shires on an English farm.

Left Shire-type showing working harness.

Opposite A pair of black Shires on a farm near Chiddingford, Surrey.

mentary, commenting that they had strong legs, good hoofs, were deep ribbed, and were willing workers, but that it seemed not to matter that some of them were 'fowle or ill-favoured'.

Between the Elizabethan age and the time of Cromwell the most significant development in heavy-horse breeding was the plan to drain the Fens. Work began in the middle of the 17th century, but was not completed until the 19th, a time of special significance for the Shire Horse.

It was Cromwell himself, in all probability, who gave the new and subsequently much-used name to the heavy horses of his age. He called them 'Blacks' and although he was almost certainly referring to Frisians, and not to the English cart or draught horse, the name passed into common usage, and the Great Horse passed into history. For the next 100 years little progress was made in improving transport, other than in an increase of the numbers of horses used; but significantly, perhaps, the breeding of cart horses (which were no longer used for war) passed from the aristocracy and the gentry, who had used them for that purpose, to the farmers, whose chief interest was in breeding a heavy horse solely for draught purposes. The breeding of the best of the 'Blacks' was centred on the Fens and adjoining areas such as Leicestershire and Staffordshire, and extending into Derbyshire. At the same time, of course, in East Anglia the Suffolk was well-established, and these two were the principal types of heavy horse in Britain. The Black, however, was still not a recognisable breed, but rather a collection of different types.

It is in the middle of the 18th century that, at last, a single horse can be named as the first stallion of importance in what was to become the Shire breed. He was known as the Packington Blind Horse, and lived between the years of 1755 and 1770, approximately, in the village of Packington near Ashby-de-la-Zouche. He was a black horse, with a white face and hairless lips and muzzle, and he is mentioned in the first Shire Stud Book, chiefly because of horses that were said to be his descendants – but details are scant.

Descriptions of the heavy horses up until this period are in short supply, other than in the most general terms, although some idea of their appearance has been gained from paintings – where allowance must always be made for a certain amount of artistic licence, and the requirement to please the rider. However, by the end of the 18th century it

A Shire-type of former years – compare with one of today's champions opposite.

was clear that the various types of Blacks that existed could be differentiated largely on account of the areas in which they were bred. They could be divided into two very different main types – those bred in the Fens, and those bred in the Midlands. In his invaluable history of the Shire horse, Keith Chivers explains that some of these differences were due to the soil differences in the two areas, the Derbyshire limestone producing hard, fine bone, and the soil of the Fens encouraging huge size and weight. This resulted in the Fens horse being the heavier, coarser type of the two, with round, soft bone, and often with shallow and weak heels. It had a large head, often with a small, white star on the forehead, and a flowing mane and tail. Its feathering was profuse, with thick, wiry, frequently curly hair. The colour was sooty black, sometimes verging on grey, with white markings on the legs.

The Midland type had a finer head, which was lean and rather narrow, often with a white blaze. It had less hair, flintier, better bone, and was a less cumbersome animal. In Derbyshire and Leicestershire these horses were nearly always black, but in Staffordshire they were predominantly brown.

The distribution of hair was also an indication of the horse's origins. Lincolnshire horses, for instance, had long moustaches, which were black in black-skinned animals. Another type had bald lips, muzzle and eyelids, while a third had a tuft of hair growing from the front of each knee, quite distinct from the normal feathering, and in some cases they also had a tuft growing from the point of the hock.

While Britain had been busy developing her heavy horses (based, of course, on European blood), Europe had been engaged in the Napoleonic Wars, and at the end of those, quite suddenly, the whole of Europe seemed to want British (or at least English) horses. This, coupled with the post-war farming slump which had been followed by a boom, led to breeding standards falling badly; while farms needed more horses than ever before, the vast majority that were being bred were appalling specimens, with dreadful legs, unwieldy and coarse. But, as so often happens in a crisis in the horse world, a few dedicated breeders managed to keep better quality animals, and retained a nucleus from which to breed better stock. So it was with the cart horses. A small number of breeders in the Fens and the Midlands (especially the former) kept up the standard, and throughout the 19th century horses from that area were spread over much of the rest of England.

A present-day champion at the British Shire Show.

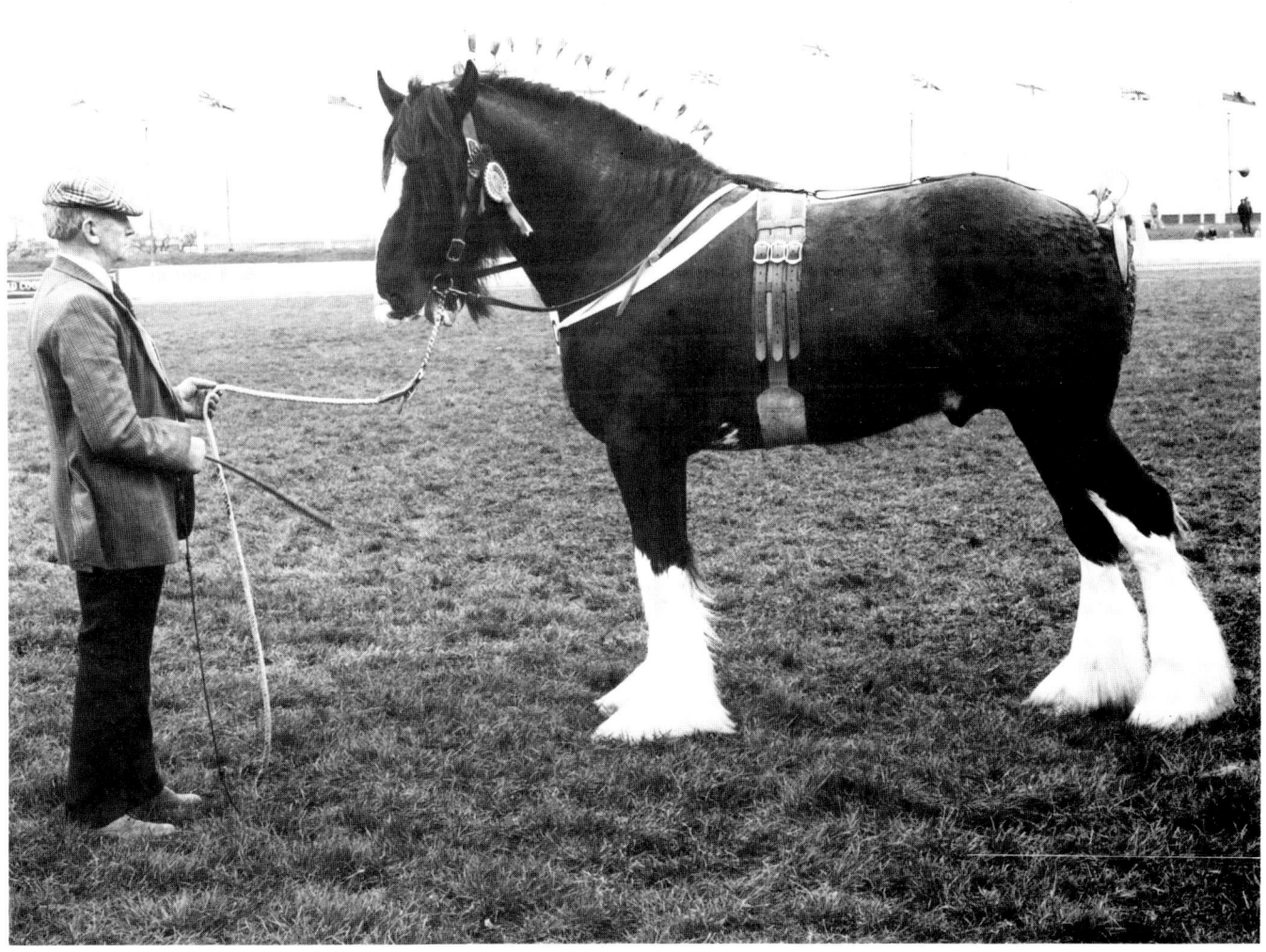

Left *A working Shire engaged in carting mangolds in England.*

Opposite *'Sleep after toil.'* (Edmund Spenser)

Consequently, as Keith Chivers points out, 'almost every good specimen of a modern pedigree Shire in the twentieth century is traceable in the direct male line to one or two horses bred in the Fens.'

During the 19th century, the variety of uses to which heavy horses were put had widened considerably. They not only worked on farms, they also pulled carts and drays in towns and cities, toiled as canal horses and, as we have seen, they were commonly referred to as 'cart horses' – the Shire was still in the future. But, let there be no mistake, the story so far told is that of the history of the modern Shire under a variety of different names.

The cart horses had survived, more or less, the arrival of the railways, and had even benefited from them to some degree. Stallions could be travelled by rail, and thus breeders in some of the more far-flung corners of England (and Wales) were able to make use of quality stallions to which they would otherwise not have had access.

In the last quarter of the 19th century English breeders were beginning, albeit slowly, to follow the Scottish practice of stallion hiring societies, which had done a great deal to improve the Clydesdale north of the border. Apart from a small group which hired a stallion in the High Peak district in 1822, the first society south of the border to embark on a scheme similar to the Scottish was, ironically, in the Welsh county of Montgomeryshire. This was the start of a very successful method in which quality stallions were hired for the breeding season by a group of breeders – a method that has lasted, with modifications and improvements, to the present day.

It might also be said that the introduction of hiring associations pushed cart-horse breeders in the direction of setting up a stud book – as selection committees entrusted with the responsibility of hiring suitable stallions not only wanted to see the animal itself, but required some reliable indications of its ability as a sire. In addition, the Suffolk and Clydesdale breeders were both known to be forming stud book societies, and the English cart-horse breeders did not greatly desire to be outdone by their competitors. As Captain Henry Heaton, manager of the Earl of Ellesmere's estates and cart-horse stud, remarked at the meeting in 1878, which had been called to discuss the possibility of such a society for the English cart horse:

> I fear that unless something is done, our Scotch friends will completely knock our legs from under us. English agriculturists ought to set up a stud-book as soon as possible, to prevent Clydesdale breeders from claiming purity for their breed over that of the Shire.

This meeting was of great significance, not only because it led to the setting-up of a committee to form a stud book association, but also because it was possibly the first in which the English cart horse was consistently referred to as 'Shire-bred'. In addition, as the Earl of Ellesmere was invited to become president of the society which was to be formed.

After some discussion about the naming of the society – some preferring 'The Cart Horse Society' and others 'The Old English Cart Horse Society' – a typically English compromise resulted in the new society, formed in April, 1878, being named 'The English Cart Horse Society'. George Mumford Sexton was secretary, and among the committee members were Sir Walter Gilbey, Mr Edward Coke and Mr Frederick Street. Most important of all, the Prince of Wales was persuaded to become Patron – the first in a long line of Royal holders of the position.

The Society's first and most important task was to prepare the stud book; it was agreed that the first volume should be retrospective and restricted to stallions foaled not later than 1876. Two years after the formation of the Society, and on the second day of the newly inaugurated Cart Horse Show at the Agricultural Hall in Islington, the first volume was available. It contained the records of 2,365 stallions and this, together with the show (the first of many that were to keep the breed in the public eye until the outbreak of the Second World War), gave the breed the status it so badly needed.

Having achieved this status, the Society, after much argument, decided to change its name to 'The Shire Horse Society' in 1884 – a name it has retained ever since. The breed went from strength to strength, competing in prestigious classes at the important agricultural shows, with exhibits improving in quality and the heavy-topped youngsters with poor legs, which had been a disturbing feature of earlier shows, no longer being accepted. The 1885 London show was noteworthy chiefly because Mr John Rowell's Prince William (son of another great horse, William the Conqueror) won the championship as a two year old, going on to win again in 1888. Another son, Staunton Hero, won the following year, and in 1887, Harold, bred by Mr J. H. Potter (a member of the same family as Mr W. H. Potter, breeder of Prince William) won; in 1890 another son of William the Conqueror, Hitchin Conqueror, was champion. These great horses were of special significance to the newly named breed, and by the outbreak of the Second World War the majority of stallions were descended from these two blood lines, with Harold's line dominating.

The years between 1901 and 1914 have been called the Golden Age of the heavy horse in Britain, and particularly of the Shire. The Society's membership had risen to 4,200 by the beginning of the war and, although it is hard to grasp these days, over 5,000 animals were registered in the stud book *each year*. But, despite its eminence, all was not wholly well with the breed. Legs were becoming exceedingly hairy and, almost inevitably, this hairiness was covering a multitude of 'leggy' sins. It was little consolation to know that the Clydesdale was at the same time losing his middle-piece and becoming increasingly tubular. The export market had by this time become a major force in Shire breeding, but overseas buyers, notably those in the highly profitable North American Market, were beginning to prefer the less hairy Clydesdales and (more than either of them) the clean-legged Percherons. While home buyers might be prepared to put up with the skin condition known as 'grease' which frequently occurred under the hair, overseas buyers were not; but it was not until the 1930s that a determined effort was made to produce cleaner-legged animals.

The Great War, of course, saw enormous losses among heavy horses of all breeds; once again but for the diligence of a few breeders, who appreciated the necessity of retaining, so far as was possible under difficult conditions, good breeding stock, the Shire must have disappeared. By 1919 some of the big shows were being held again, and in 1920, the great Field Marshal, owned by that staunch and enthusiastic owner and breeder of Shires, King George V, won the junior championship at the London show and, amid scenes of great excitement and rejoicing, went on to take the supreme championship.

But the triumphant re-emergence of the heavy horse was comparatively short-lived and in the 1920s, the increasing dominance of the internal combustion engine was matched by the decline of the horse in its traditional roles. Even a temporary reprieve during the Second World War could not halt the inevitable and by 1947, even pedigree stock was finishing up in the knackers' yards.

This time all but the most committed of breeders must have felt that the end of the Shire was approaching, but heavy-horse men (and women) are a stubborn race, and a few managed to hang on – just. Things were difficult: government grants to hiring societies were stopped in 1957 (having been in operation since before the war), and this sounded the death knell for a number of them; the Horserace Betting Levy Board, begun as the Racecourse Totalisator Charity Trust in the late 1920s cut its grant to the hiring societies completely, and reduced the amount for the Shire Horse Society. The number of entries for shows declined, and heavy horses all over the country – not just the Shires – appeared to be on the verge of total destruction.

However, for no clearly defined reason – perhaps something as simple as a reaction against the pace of modern life – the breed enjoyed a tiny revival in the early 1960s. Breweries were using the horses for publicity purposes, the Drive of the Heavy Horses at London's Horse of the Year Show, seen on television by thousands, renewed public interest, and, of vital importance, Mr Roy Bird became breed society secretary, on the retirement in 1962 of Mr Albert Holland, who had done so much for the breed during his years in office. Slowly but surely the revival gathered strength.

The Shire Horse Society celebrated its 90th birthday in 1968, an event marked by a marathon drive from the Society's headquarters in Peterborough to Buckingham Palace, organised by the President, Mr David Kay. The numbers in heavy-horse classes were increasing again, and heavy horse centres, most of them with Shires in residence, were being established by private individuals and breweries in various parts of the country, and were (and most certainly still are) attracting large crowds. Membership of the Society increased, as did the numbers of horses and the entries in the stud book. The 'new-style' Shire, with the emphasis once more on the cleaner-legged horse, was on the up and up; and the export trade, although but a trickle

A sight to gladden a Shire-man's heart! The Grand Finale to the Shire Horse Society's Centenary Show, attended by Her Majesty the Queen and H.R.H. the Duke of Edinburgh. The Queen is the Society's Patron.

compared with the early days of the century, was reviving, with horses being sent to the United States, Canada and Australia.

In 1973, the Society established a stallion premium scheme, offering premiums worth some hundreds of pounds to selected stallions, which are inspected at the annual show at Peterborough each spring. Hiring societies

are now operating in a number of areas – and the future looks more assured. The Shire Horse Society entered its second century with confidence and the belief that, while heavy horses will never again be used in such numbers as during the late 19th and early 20th centuries, they are no longer to be regarded as the near-forgotten relics of a bygone age.

One of the most satisfying manifestations of the revival of interest in heavy horses has undoubtedly been the renewed export trade. The first Shires were exported to the United States in 1883, and from then until the American depression of the 1890s, the flood-gates were opened, hundreds of horses being shipped across the Atlantic. The American Shire Horse Society was formed in 1885. But, as with the Clydesdales, a great number of very poor specimens were 'off-loaded', as well as some very good ones. Principal importer of *good* Shires was John Truman, whose name will always be linked with the introduction of the breed to the United States. After the depression, exports started again, though not on anything like the same scale; however, the horses were, on average, of much better quality. But the mini-boom was short-lived – and this can be attributed to just one thing. The Americans did not like the excessive amount of hair on the Shires' legs and, as has been recounted in earlier pages, the Shires lost the market.

Australia, too, in the first ten years of this century, imported numbers of Shires, initially into Tasmania, Victoria and New South Wales, and later into Queensland. The Australians also sent Shires across the Tasman Sea to New Zealand – notably the the stallion King of Kings, who went from Tasmania, and the Australian-born daughters of a horse called Lincolnshire Hero. For reasons which will become apparent, however, the Shires proved unsuitable for Australian working conditions, and although they were used to cross with Clydesdales and Percherons to produce lighter draught-horses more suited to the environment, the export trade dwindled and came to a virtual standstill. Shires were registered, together with Clydesdales and the Shire/Clydesdale cross, up until about 1912, after which registrations appear to have lapsed.

Nothing further was done until 1978, when the present Shirehorse Society of Australia was formed. (The Society is named 'Shirehorse' because of the possible confusion arising with an Australian 'Shire' which is a local government electoral division.) The secretary of the Society, Grahame A. West, in a very interesting account, explains that there are few Shires left in Australia because the majority of the early imports were at a disadvantage in the tropics (and even in southern Australia it can be exceedingly hot in summer). They sweated profusely from their large surface area, and so lost energy rapidly. Their extreme hairiness was an added problem, as the very fine feathers attracted insects of various kinds, and in any case they did not stand up to the torrential rain of the cyclone season in the north as well as breeds with coarser hair. The Clydesdales, which were smaller, lighter and generally less hairy, lost less condition in the heat and so survived in appreciable numbers. The only Shires to survive were the lighter ones, which Mr West describes as being more like the modern English Shire, but more of a walking type, short in the leg, but with coarser hair, and not so good-looking.

At present there are probably only about forty Shires in Australia, of which Mr West owns about ten, and Mr Bernd Ulrich around twenty. One of the principal problems facing Australian breeders is the presence of a tick (known as scrub tick or shell-back tick) which kills foals unless they are treated with spray every few days, and sometimes even kills fully grown horses.

Another difficulty, of course, is the very small numbers, and while acknowledging that to improve the breed local breeders will have to inbreed and line-breed and cull, there is a feeling that (in spite of the obvious objections) a properly regulated horse-meat trade would be helpful so that culled animals could be disposed of profitably.

With the establishment of the new society came the decision to recognise two types of Shire in Australia – the Modern (the rangier, clean-legged variety) and the Traditional (heavier with more feathering), and it is intended to register them separately in the newly founded stud book.

The Soviet Heavy Draught See RUSSIAN HEAVY BREEDS.

A pair of Shires at work during harvest time. The shortage of horse 'gears' (machinery) may impede the return of more heavies to modern agriculture.

The Suffolk

For the greater part of 500 years, the most unmistakable of the British heavy horses, the Suffolk Punch, has been a recognised part of the English rural scene, and for much of that time it has existed in a form that bears at least some resemblance to the present-day horse. It thus has the distinction of being the oldest established breed of British draught horse, and furthermore, it is unique in that every animal alive today can trace its ancestry back in a single unbroken line to a horse that was foaled in 1768 (the year that Captain Cook set sail in *Endeavour*). Throughout its long history, and even today, the Suffolk's chief breeding area has been the county from which it takes its name.

It is also unique in that the breed has, for 100 years or more, existed only in seven shades of 'chesnut' (the traditional Suffolk spelling). These shades range from a dark brown, mahogany or liver, through dull-dark, mealy, red, golden, lemon, and bright, with the latter being the most popular and the most numerous.

In appearance the modern Suffolk fits its well-known 'Punch' image – the dictionary definition of 'punch' being 'a variety of English horse, short-legged and barrel-bodied, a short, fat fellow'. It is *so* distinctive in appearance and, if only because of its colour, cannot possibly be mistaken for any other of the British heavies. Apart from the colour, its proportions are characteristic: 'long, low, and wide' with very short legs carrying no feathering, an exceptionally deep, well-ribbed up body, well-rounded and muscular quarters, and a markedly low-set shoulder which enables it to throw most of its not inconsiderable weight into the collar to great advantage. The Suffolk's walk is smart, with a balanced, slightly swinging action, and its trot, which differs in cadence from that of the Shire and the Clydesdale, has been described most aptly by Adrian Bell as 'a tense, slow trot as though to ease an overflow of strength'. There should be a certain amount of knee action, but no Suffolk judge 'delights in seeing a horse lift his knees up to his throat latch'. Plaiting is considered a serious defect by Suffolk judges, but some believe that the breed's very wide front is bound to lead to a degree of dishing – however, this should not be pronounced. Similarly, there is a good width between the forelegs, but the hind feet must be close together, and a Suffolk should be able to perform his traditional work of walking up a 9 in. (23 cm.) furrow easily. As one judge pointed out, 'if a horse has too much width between his hocks, and is going between rows of sugar beet, he'll kick out more than he'll hoe' – so there are, as always, practical considerations to most points of conformation.

Looking at the conformation in more detail, the Suffolk's head is large, intelligent-looking, often with a white blaze. The forehead is wide, and the eyes full and bright. The neck is deep and tapering, and the shoulders strong and well-muscled. The chest is wide and the body exceptionally deep, giving plenty of room for heart and lungs, while the back is wide and level, the quarters strong with a good breeching, and a well-set tail. The forearms are strong, the knees big and flat, and the cannons markedly short, free of hair, and with adequate hard, flat bone, leading to pasterns that slope at the same angle as the hoof. The latter is strong, open, and wide a large frog and a good width of heel. The gaskins are strong, and the hocks flat and free from coarseness. The modern Suffolk mare stands about 16 to 16.2 hands (162.6 to 167.6 cm.) and the stallions 17 to 17.1 hands (172.8 to 175.3 cm.) – rather larger than in the past, but those who prefer the larger horse insist that the height should come from the depth of the body and *not* from increased length of leg.

Throughout its history the Suffolk has been noted for its great draught power, and from at least the 18th century, descriptions exist of various tests and competitions held to demonstrate the breed's strength. In his book *Ask the Fellows Who Cut the Hay*, George Ewart Evans tells of one of the old horse fairs held in a Suffolk village up until the end of the last century. The fair was attended by horse dealers from all over the country, including some from London who were looking for horses to draw the great wagons of flour from the docks to the warehouses.

Horse dealers take nothing on trust, and they required their prospective purchases to demonstrate their ability as draught horses before buying them. First of all (in a test that appears to have been unique to Suffolk) a horse would be hitched to a large fallen tree, and the dealers would assess his pulling power. He would not be expected to move the tree, but any Suffolk that did not, in his attempts to move it, get right down on his knees in the manner typical of the breed, would not pass the test. (In the 14th century illustrated manuscript, the Luttrell Salter, the lead horse of a team is shown in this attitude.)

The second test involved harnessing the horse to a vehicle and requiring it to back some distance. For draught work in towns this was a necessary skill, and a number of animals apparently could not bear the unaccustomed feel of the breeching strap against their hind legs as they reined back – a manoeuvre that a plough horse (which most of them were) would not normally be required to perform.

On a lighter note (for the spectators but certainly not for the horses), the 18th century saw many 'drawing matches', where wagers were laid on teams of horses' ability to pull a dead weight over a given distance – clearly the forerunners of the great pulling tests that are now so popular in America, and are also gaining ground in Australia. Training for these events was just as enthusiastic then as now. Ewart Evans quotes from the 18th century writer, Arthur Young:

They [the Suffolk horses] are all taught with very great care to draw in concert, and many farmers are so attentive to this point that they have teams, every horse of which will fall on his knees at the word of command twenty times running in the full drawing attitude, and all at the same moment; but without exerting any strength till a variation in the word orders them to give all their strength; and then they will carry amazing weight. It is common to draw team against team for high wagers.

The Reverend Sir John Cullum described the actual competition:

The trial is made with a wagon loaded with sand, the wheels sunk a little into the ground, with blocks of wood laid before them to increase the difficulty. The first efforts are made with the reins fastened as usual to the collar; but the animals cannot, when so confined, put out their full strength; the reins are therefore afterwards thrown loose on their necks, when they can exert their utmost powers, which they usually do by falling on their knees, and drawing in that attitude. That they may not break their knees in this operation, the area on which they draw is strewn with soft sand.

A considerable amount is known about the more recent history of the Suffolk horse, but in common with the other breeds of British heavies, the precise origins are impossible to trace with any certainty. William Youatt, in the classic book *The Horse*, published in 1831, asserts that it resulted from crosses between imported Norman (? Percheron) stallions and local (Suffolk) cart mares. Be that as it may, the first known reference to the breed was made in 1586 by William Camden in *Brittania*, in which he mentions its existence as far back as 1506. Little if anything further is heard about it as a breed until the mid-18th century, by which time various descriptions make it clear that it had developed into a recognisable, although by some accounts less than beautiful, breed.

The Reverend Sir John Cullum, writing in 1784, described it as:

... a most useful breed of that noble animal, not indeed peculiar to this parish, but I believe to the county. The breed is well known by the name of Suffolk Punches. They are generally about 15 hands high, of a remarkable short and compact make; their legs bony and their shoulders loaded with flesh. Their colour is often of light sorrel (chesnut), which is as much remembered in some distant parts of the kingdom as their form ... for draught they are perhaps unrivalled as for their gentle and tractable temper; and to exhibit proofs of their great power ...

It seems likely that the Reverend Cullum was describing the breed as it was at that time, when breeders were apparently trying to produce a more handsome, lighter and active animal. This can be inferred from the writings of Arthur Young at about the same time who, in contrast, refers disparagingly to 'the old breed':

An etching showing a stylised representation of a Suffolk at the beginning of the 19th century.

I remember seeing many of the old breed, which were very famous, and, in some respects, an uglier horse could not be viewed; sorrel-colour, very low in the fore-end, a large ill-shaped head, with slouching heavy ears, a great carcase and short legs, but short-backed... These horses could only walk and draw; they could trot no better than a cow. But their drawing power was considerable. Of late years, by aiming at coach-horses, the breed is much changed to a handsomer, lighter and more active horse.

However, in spite of its earlier ill-favoured appearance, the horse had been carefully bred to suit the needs of the East Anglian farmers, who had to work the very heavy clay soils of the area. Indeed, it is claimed that Suffolks are the only British draught horse to be developed solely for agriculture. Tucked away in their relatively isolated breeding centres, the Suffolk men had paid rather less attention than other heavy-horse breeders to the requirement of 17th century England for war horses. They had concentrated on producing their breed with its remarkably low shoulder, which was eminently suited for draught work; and they were probably assisted in this by the early enclosing of that part of England, which more or less eliminated the indiscriminate breeding that had been rife under the open field system of agriculture. But, as we have seen, by the last quarter of the 18th century, some were beginning to modify their ideas to produce animals which could 'double' as coach horses, and Sir John Cullum himself used them during his journeying round North Wales. It does seem, therefore, that the breed was in the process of changing – and had in fact *already* changed to some extent, and this continued, with the breeders very skilfully managing to retain the Suffolks' great strength and draught power, while improving its overall conformation.

It was the latter part of the 18th century that could truly be called the formative period of the Suffolk breed. From that period, Herman Biddell, who in the *next* century was responsible for the monumental work of compiling volume one of the stud book, named five lines of horses who exerted great influence on the breed, although in due course all merged into one principal line. The most influential, in terms of the breed's subsequent history, was the stallion foaled in 1768, and owned by Thomas Crisp. It was known as Thomas Crisp's Horse of Ufford 404 (the figure being the stud book number). Biddell wrote that this animal must be thought of as having 'a low fore-end, large carcase, short legs and bent hocks, and perhaps a less inelegant head than most of his contemporaries'. As a five-year-old, this bright chestnut, standing just 15.2 hands (157.5 cm.), was advertised as 'able to get good stock for coach or road', and he travelled as a stallion in the Woodbridge, Saxmundham and Framlingham area – the heart of Suffolk country. (There has always been a mystery about Thomas Crisp and where he lived, but recent research by author and historian, Norman Scarfe, has shed some light on the problem. He searched the Ufford Parish records in vain for any Crisp living at the relevant time. He now suggests that the title 'Crisp's Horse of *Ufford*' is a

A pair of Suffolks at work during harvest in Norfolk, England.

mistake, and that it should be 'Crisp's Horse of Orford', as a family named Crisp lived at Gedgrave Hall, Orford, and had a stud of Suffolk horses at that time.)

An early infusion of 'outside' blood came with a horse called Farmer 174 that headed the 'Blake Tribe' – so called because it was owned by Andrew Blake. Farmer had no true Suffolk blood in him at all, being a chestnut Lincoln trotting horse. Blake crossed him with Suffolks and so founded a line of neat, compact horses that lasted for nearly a century before finally dying out.

Another line was founded by a half-bred Suffolk, Farmer's Glory, who produced tall, angular horses, with very heavy bone – a line known as the Attleborough tribe, which finally ended about 1880. Biddell describes another strain, introduced about the same time, and stemming from Barber's Proctor 58 who, although a bay himself, produced a line of dark chestnuts, many of whom were lacking in bone, and a bit 'on the leg'. The last of the five lines was founded by a horse called Samson 324.

All these horses are of importance, in that they contributed to improving the breed, but their lines died out and the Crisp line became dominant. By 1952, the then secretary of the Suffolk Horse Society was able to write, 'Every animal now in existence traces its descent in the direct male line to Crisp's Horse of Ufford.'

In any account of the Suffolk breed the name of Herman Biddell, compiler of volume one of the stud book, stands head and shoulder above any other individual, and the book he produced has rightly been described as 'a classic among livestock books'.

Since the 1840s, the more astute breeders had realised that if the Suffolk was to prosper, and breeding be conducted in anything other than the relatively haphazard manner which was commonplace at the time, some form of registry of pedigrees was necessary. As early as 1850 one of the larger stud owners, Nathanial Barthropp, had started a stud book, but this was never completed, and it was not until 1862 (twenty or thirty years too late, as he acknowledged) that Herman Biddell, a local farmer with a lifelong interest in the breed, invited to his home a gathering of the most knowledgeable 'horse-leaders' in the county. (A horse-leader was the groom who, in those days, led a stallion around a prescribed district to cover mares that were brought to him') Biddell appreciated that these men, whose memories for horses and their progeny was phenomenal, and in some cases reached back fifty or sixty years, were going to be his chief source of accurate information. He also collected as many stud cards, sale catalogues, and stallion advertisements as he could lay his hands on, and following the success of the initial meeting of horse-leaders, he held others. During the following three years he also visited many farms and studs, and searched the county for information he knew must be in existence. He also sought information from adjoining counties, and in due course accumulated a mass of facts, which he then set about analysing and arranging into book form. When it was published in 1880 entitled *The Suffolk Horse History and Stud Book*, it was, in fact, far more than that, as it included a fascinating history of general farming in Suffolk at that time. It contained a history of the breed, a register of 1,230 stallions and 1,120 mares, a marvellous description of an ideal Suffolk, and some excellent drawings of outstanding examples of the breed, as well as a list of prize-winners going back to at least the year 1840.

The publishing of the stud book was one of the first achievements of the Suffolk Stud Book Association, which was founded in 1877, with Herman Biddell as its first secretary. It was the first of the heavy horse breed societies founded in Britain. Throughout its existence, the Society has endeavoured to maintain and improve the quality of the Suffolk horse. One of its earliest schemes was designed to help the small farmer keep mares and have them served by quality stallions. It was known as the Breeding Scheme; it began in 1897, and continued until 1951.

Under this scheme, the Society bought a number of mares, costing not more than 60 gns., and passed them on to a limited number of small farmers. The farmers in turn paid not less than a quarter of the original purchase price, and also four per cent interest on the balance (which had been paid for by the Society). The farmer was entitled to work the mare, and she was also put to one of the Society's nominated stallions each year. The farmer then reared the foal, and in due course returned it to the Society, who paid him £16 10s. for it.

Another scheme was introduced when the number of horses on the land dropped dramatically with the introduction of tractors. When this happened, many of the older horsemen also left, and the young ones knew little of horse-management, so the farmers who still bred horses found they were short of skilled labour. In an effort to encourage farmers to continue breeding and using Suffolks, the Society established a breaking-in centre for youngstock. Here an experienced handler, or 'horse-gentler' as he is called in Suffolk (so much more appropriate than a horse-breaker), would take the youngsters in hand, accustom them to wearing a halter, and to being led and, finally, school them 'to all gears' – that is, teach them how to work in harness with ploughs, harrows, etc. They would then be returned to the owner.

Both these schemes have, of course, now been discontinued as official Society policy. It is interesting, however, that enthusiasm for heavy horses has now revived to such an extent that there is again a demand for people to break horses to farm gear, a task which Roger Clark, a well-known Suffolk breeder, does with great skill at his farm at Stoke-by-Nayland in Suffolk.

Perhaps the most important and far-reaching step taken by the Society was to eliminate bad feet, and more particularly side-bone, which was prevalent in the breed. (Side-bone is an hereditary condition of the foot in which the cartilages become ossified; this leads to a lack of elasticity in the foot, and to almost certain lameness.) In a determined effort to stamp out this condition the Society introduced, in the late 19th century, veterinary inspections for all animals at shows, and any suggestion of sidebone automatically led to disqualification from awards. By this means sidebone in the breed was eliminated, but the Society still attaches so much importance to good feet that at the annual breed show special prizes are still awarded for horses that are judged to have the best feet. So, from being a breed that was regarded with some suspicion as far as its feet were concerned, the Suffolk is now well-known for its soundness in that respect.

The present-day Society is very active in promoting the breed in various ways, and has recently started a premium scheme to encourage the breeding and rearing of good young colts and the retention of older stallions for breeding purposes. Premiums of £50 are to be awarded to each stallion forward at the breed show, with an extra £150 to be awarded by a judge's panel to stallions of sufficient merit. To encourage showing in harness, the Society is offering grants to farmer-owned four-horse teams at some of the major agricultural shows. In addition, in an endeavour to ensure that stallions are available for members who require a mare to be served, the Society is giving grants to a number of owners whose stallions have been accepted either to travel or to stand at stud during the season.

Suffolks have always been renowned as 'good doers', or in more modern terms 'good converters', of food, and have the reputation of needing less food than other comparable breeds. This had some effect on the hours they worked in the fields. A typical working day for a Suffolk on a farm would begin at about 4.30 a.m., with the morning feed or 'bait', and grooming. Two full hours were allowed for this, as no responsible horseman would allow less for his horse to digest his food properly. At 6.30 a.m., the horse would be led out to the fields to work, which he would do with short rest periods interspersed; but, in contrast to most other heavy breeds, who would have a mid-morning nosebag, he would have no more food until he returned to the stable at about 2.30 p.m. The horses were then groomed, fed, and eventually bedded down for the night at about 5.30 p.m. – or in some districts they might, if the weather was suitable, be turned out into a straw-strewn yard, or into the fields. This time-table was known as a 'one-yoke shift'. Other farms (perhaps those that did not use all Suffolks) might have worked a 'two-yoke shift', starting at the same time, but at about mid-morning, the horses would be brought back to the stable for a proper feed and a rest before returning for up to three hours more work in the afternoon.

Suffolks are, as has been shown, primarily agricultural animals, although they were also used as city draught animals in London, and are now used for publicity purposes by breweries. But one of their most interesting present-day tasks has been at the Hollesley Bay Borstal and Detention Centre on the Suffolk coast. Here the horses, which in addition to being part of the oldest and largest Suffolk stud in the world (the 'Colony' prefix is renowned), work in the centre's farm, and play a very important role in the training and rehabilitation of the young offenders who are sent to Hollesley.

The Colony extends over some 1,400 acres, of which about 1,100 are farmed – crops include potatoes, fruit, mixed vegetables, grass and glasshouse crops; there is a dairy herd of 450; and, at the time of writing, there are over thirty Suffolk horses.

There are two stallions, and the remainder are mares for breeding purposes and a few geldings for working. The work force of the stud consists of a groom and six to eight trainees (as the boys are called). About 95 per cent of the boys who actually work with the horses have never had anything to do with animals before, but they have expressed a wish to spend their time at Hollesley working on the stud. Mr John Bramley, the estate manager (and the present Chairman of the Suffolk Horse Society) finds that the more inarticulate boys tend to gravitate towards the stud, and within a very short time the staff notice a difference in them, and are convinced that the newly found

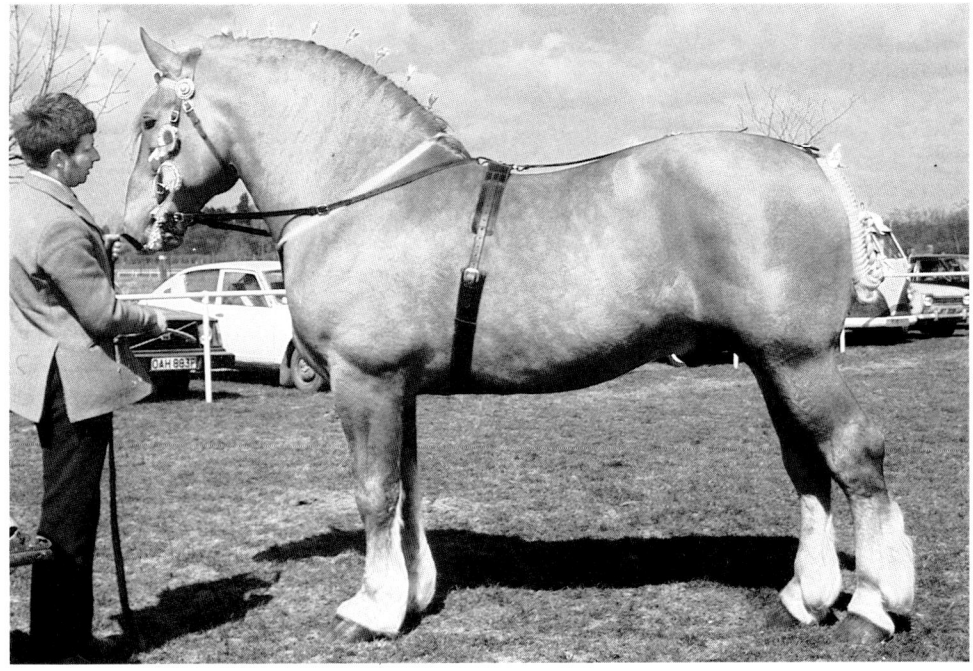

Mr and Mrs Roger Clark's superb champion stallion, Rowhedge Count. Sadly, this handsome Suffolk died when struck by lightning.

responsibility of looking after animals is of great benefit.

Naturally enough, the trainees do not start looking after the horses right from the start – they begin, as most people coming into the horse world for the first time, by doing the more menial work, such as harness cleaning and mucking out the stables. In this way the trainees become accustomed to being with the horses, and when a boy has sufficient confidence to go into the stall and stand beside the horse without being frightened, he is moved on to the next stage, learning how to groom and progressing from there. One of the daily tasks for the horses is pulling the rubbish cart round the farm, and two trainees are usually employed on this. As the estate manager remarked, 'The horse knows more about the job than anyone else,' but the trainees get enormous satisfaction from feeling that they can manage the animal. As the boys progress they move on to taking the stallions out for their walk.

The Colony stud is a very busy showing stable during the season, and the boys are fully involved in this. They learn to braid the animals for showing, and the groom takes the number of boys he thinks he will need to the show. They do not actually *show* the horses themselves, solely because this is regarded as a professional job and the boys do not have enough experience, but they do handle the horses in parades which are not competitive. Recently four of them took part in a display that has not been seen since before the Second World War. They harnessed four horses in line to a cart and, with a boy at the head of each, performed a walking version of the Royal Horse Artillery's musical drive. The staff notice that after having been to shows, the trainees' attitude is considerably modified; they lose much of their aggression, and anti-authority outlook.

The trainees are also closely involved in stud work, and they learn to use the stallions on the mares and, if it is possible, they help when the mares are foaling. The basis of the work with the horses (as indeed with the whole farm) is to teach the trainees that work is an integral part of life and that it can be satisfying and rewarding. Especially with the horses, they learn to accept responsibility. When they are given a horse to look after, they learn that the animal is dependent on them for feeding and watering, and general care.

The success of the scheme may be judged by the fact that many of the trainees, after they have been allocated to various other jobs on the farm, are inclined to ask for a change after about a month. This seldom happens when they are working with the horses, and one or two boys have even asked if they could stay on after they are officially due to leave. Over the years, a few have gone on to find work with horses after they have left Hollesley Bay.

Suffolks are numerically a small breed, and only a few are used for farming in Britain these days. Over the years some have been exported. For instance, Pakistan has from time to time taken a number and used them for breeding army horses, and recently, one of the Colony horses has been sold to Italy for use in breeding show jumpers and eventers. A young stallion has just been bought by the Danish Jutland Horse Society to use on the mares to improve the breed – the Jutland is, as has been seen, not unlike a small Suffolk. The United States is once again entering the buying field; there appears to be a revival of demand, particularly for fillies under two years of age, and the United States Suffolk Horse breed society is flourishing. In the early years of this century, a few Suffolks found their way out to Australia, and, as described, played at least some part in the foundation of what is now the Australian Draught Horse.

The breed's future in Britain seems assured, especially if the present renewed interest in heavy horses continues. There is always a demand for heavyweight hunters in this country, and the Suffolk has been, and still is, used to some extent for crossing with Thoroughbreds to produce high quality examples of this type.

The Vladimir Heavy Draught See THE RUSSIAN HEAVY BREEDS

Above Suffolks at play. These delightful horses are unmistakable because of their distinctive colour – one of the seven shades of 'chesnut' – and their proportions, that of 'a short, fat fellow'.

Opposite Line-up of Suffolks at the Breed Show in England. This breed is unique in that every animal can trace its ancestry back to a horse foaled in 1768.

Heavy-Horse Harness

There are two principal kinds of heavy-horse harness – plough harness and cart harness. There are national and regional variations, but the basic patterns are very much the same. Looking at the plough harness, the first item that goes on is the collar. This is put on upside-down and is then turned because, as can be seen, the collar is wider at the bottom than at the top, while the horse's head is not! Some collars are made with a latch at the top that can be opened, so that it can be fitted round the neck instead of over the head. In general, these are thought less satisfactory, as they are inclined to move and cause rubs on the neck and shoulders.

In Scotland, and in parts of the United States, a very distinctive high-peaked collar (known as the Scottish Peaked Collar) is sometimes used – possibly more often in cart than in ploughing harness, and in some European countries, for instance, Hungary, a breast collar is used. This is a broad piece of leather that goes across the horse's chest, at such a height that its top touches the junction of the neck and the shoulder; it is kept in position by a neck

Left   A Shire in full decorated harness for a harness decoration class.

Opposite, bottom A team of decorated Clydesdales at the Royal Show, Stoneleigh.

strap. Draught hooks are attached to the harness at the shoulder.

Next, on harness with a collar, comes the hames. These are curved pieces of metal (or more rarely, wood) which fit into a groove round the collar, and bear at their top ends (which stand up above the horses back) the rings for the ploughlines or reins, and, at the appropriate level on the shoulders, the hook for the plough chains. Then comes the bridle – there are a variety of these. They may be open (i.e., without blinkers), but the majority tend to be 'closed', with blinkers. They may be 'full-faced', with a broad piece of leather joining the head strap by way of the brow band to the nosestrap, or they may be made without. The bridle, of course, carries the bit, which may be either fixed or hooked. If fixed, the bit must be slipped into the horse's mouth as the bridle is put over the head, but if it is hooked, it can be fitted when the bridle is on, and unhooked to slip it out of the horse's mouth during the day when it has a nosebag. Once the bridle is on, the throat lash is done up to help keep it in place. The bearing reins are attached to the bit rings and are usually just looped over the top of the hames to stop the horse putting its head down when working. Most horsemen finish by putting on the back band and the crupper strap. The latter, made with a loop, goes under the horse's tail and buckles to the top of the collar; the back band hangs down each side of the body, so that the trace chains can be attached to it, and it is sometimes made to encircle the girth completely, by the addition of a belly band. Some horse's also have a hip strap, and the trace chains are also attached to these.

When harnessing ready to draw a vehicle, the collar, hames and bridle are put on in a similar fashion, but the rest of the procedure is slightly different. A saddle (which is really a form of pad, and does not resemble a riding saddle) is put on, and secured round the horse's body with a girth, and to the collar with meeter (or metre) straps. The harnessing is then completed with the addition of the breechings, which consist of a crupper strap (attached to the back of the saddle), a loin strap, hip strap and breech band – all of which come into use to hold the cart back when going down hill. The horse is now ready to be 'shut in' to the vehicle.

Heavy Horse Harness

Bridle
a blinker
b brow band
c nose band
d cheek-strap
e head-strap
f throat-lash
g bit
h bearing rein

Collar
i forewale
j side-piece
k body (the padding)
l hames
m housen

Saddle
n saddle housing
o bridge
p pad
q girth strap
r belly band

Breechings
s crupper
t loin strap
u hip strap
v breech band

Ornate and very beautiful show harness on brewery horses in Germany.

Another example of European show harness. Continental harness is generally more showy than that of Britain.

Horses in Competition

Heavy-horse owners the world over enjoy competing with their animals in a great variety of show classes – from the straightforward but extremely important in-hand, halter, or breeding classes, through the spectacular harness classes, the pulling contests of the United States, Canada and Australia, to the more technical complexities of ploughing matches.

The preparation for a show begins long before the show season – indeed, as one season ends, the efficient exhibitor is already thinking about the next. If the horses are to be turned out for the winter, their shoes must be removed, and the feet trimmed to keep them in good shape and condition. Horses with feathers, such as Shires and Clydesdales, need special attention, and many exhibitors dress the feathers with an oily preparation, which must be repeated every month.

At the beginning of the year, the feet need trimming again, and the horse is shod at least several weeks before the start of the new season – it is no more sensible to have a horse shod immediately before a show, than for a human to wear a new pair of shoes on a cross-country hike – both types need breaking in.

Grooming for the show starts weeks before the actual date, with a really thorough grooming twice a day. If a nice warm day comes along, there is nothing better than an all-over wash with warm water and shampoo, but this cannot be done safely in cold or wet weather. The shampoo is washed off with another soaking with warm water, and the horse is very carefully dried – the best method of doing this is with a wisp, a handful of straw twisted into a convenient size and used with an energetic sweeping and thumping action.

The Percheron stallion Newstead Punch competing at an Australian Draught Pulling Contest. The champion horse pulled 3,410 lbs. – 2.77 times his own weight. This horse is well on the way to going down on his knees with the effort.

If the weather is unsuitable for an all-over shampoo, then just the legs, feet and face are washed, and again, great care is taken with drying, especially the feet, as dampness can lead to cracked or greasy heels, particularly in hairy-legged animals. This is done with wood-flour, that is, fine-ground white sawdust (and it *must* be white); or, if the ground variety is not available, ordinary dry sawdust is used. The horse's legs are stood, one at a time, on an opened-out sack or bag, and the sawdust is rubbed thoroughly into the feathering until the leg is completely dry. The remnants of the sawdust are then brushed out with a dandy brush. This treatment ensures that the legs are completely dry, but gives the feathers a beautiful texture. Clydesdale exhibitors often use resin instead of sawdust, and this fluffs the hair out a little.

Exhibitors in all classes take enormous trouble to turn their horses out looking absolutely beautiful. The least specialised (from the turn-out point of view) are the in-hand classes, in which the animals are led round the ring by the exhibitor, and are judged against the standard of perfection for their breed. Their conformation, movement and breed type is assessed. Even for these classes the preparation can take many hours. In Britain the manes and tails are braided (plaited), but in some European countries the manes are left in their natural state. In many in-hand classes it is common practice to have a neck-ribbon around the base of the neck to enhance its length.

Plaiting of the manes is not just decorative, it can, in the hands of a skilled man (or woman), make a very ordinary neck into an elegantly arched one, or give a short neck the impression of length. Plaiting of tails is also decorative, but it has a practical application in that it keeps the tails of working horses from dragging in the mud, or being caught up in the machinery or 'gears' with which they may be working, or becoming tangled in the reins.

In Britain the four breeds have developed different styles of plaiting. For instance, with Suffolks and Clydesdales a 'full-rig' plaiting is employed, in which *all* the hair of the mane is used, while with Shires and Percherons a 'half-rig' is used, in which some of the hair is left unplaited to lie on the side of the neck. Clydesdale stallions are always plaited up, but not geldings or colts under two years old when shown in hand.

The actual technicalities of plaiting, too, differ somewhat from breed to breed, though they are variations of the same basic theme. Nearly all involve the incorporation of ribbon or bass (raffia) into the plaits, and the colours of these decorations may vary from district to district, from breed to breed, and from country to country. Exhibitors also ensure that the colours enhance the colour of their horse's coat. For example, greys are often decorated with red in one part of Britain, while in another it is the custom to use blue.

Even the simplest braiding of manes and tails is an art, and being a visual, practical art, it does not translate well

Below, left *Washing a Shire's feathering before the Breed Show. It must be dried off properly.*

Below, right *Applying fine white sawdust to the legs.*

Above *A ploughing match in 1847 at Newton Abbot in Devon. Some similarities can be seen between this wood engraving and the photograph opposite of a present-day pair of Clydesdales taking part in a working of heavy horses. Note the decorative ear-muffs (which also protect the ears from insects) which can be clearly seen on the horses opposite.*

into words. However, a description of one type of 'full-rig' and one type of 'half-rig' may be of interest.

In the full-rig Suffolk plaiting, a bunch of the coloured ribbons or bass about 1 yd. (0.9 m.) long is required, and is knotted at one end. Prior to plaiting, the mane, which has already been brushed and combed carefully, is brushed over to the off-side of the neck. The bunch of bass is laid at the very top of the neck between the ears, and is secured with a few hairs of mane. Plaiting is done in the usual fashion, with three pieces of material, and as each crossing is made, a small section of mane is taken in with the bass. The plait must be tight and as neat as possible. Every 6 in. (15 cm.) a decoration such as a small flag or standard is plaited in. For a harness class the plaiting stops to allow for the collar, but for an in-hand class the full length of the mane is plaited and at the end a single piece of ribbon is tied around the end of the plait, the ends of the ribbon being trimmed straight across. There is, in the Suffolks, a slight difference in the siting of the plaits for stallions as compared with mares. The stallion's plait is positioned right on the top of the neck to emphasise the crest, and a clever plaiter can incorporate a small roll of material into a plait to enhance the crest – a practice not admired by judges. The plait of a mare is usually set slightly to one side.

An example of a half-rig is seen in the Percherons (in Britain, but not in France, where a full-rig is customary) in which the mane is still combed to one side, but only some of the hair is taken in, making a much smaller plait. For in-hand classes, up to eight standards are plaited in, while for harness classes up to ten may be used.

The braiding of tails, too, varies, as some breeds have their tails cut very short (for example, the Shires) while others, such as the Suffolks and the Percherons, are left to grow to their full length. In the Suffolk the tail is well brushed, then, starting at the top and as close as possible to the root, two small bunches of hair are taken, crossed, and brought round to the upper surface of the tail and plaited in with the bass, so that the plait runs straight down the centre. This is continued until the bottom of the dock is reached. There, the remainder of the hair is divided into three, turned back and secured with ribbon. Additional ribbons are added at intervals.

The Shire's tail is treated quite differently. In some the tail is cut short, and the dock is shaved, but in others the bulk of the tail is left at its normal length. Starting at the top, hair is taken from either side and, using plenty of bass, is plaited. Then, smaller sections of hair are taken from each side, and plaited on either side of and above the first one, again using plenty of bass, so that they stand upright like two fingers. Finally, a circular decoration, used almost exclusively for Shires, and known as a jug handle, is fastened to the first plait, and tied in with more raffia.

Coloured ribbons are added, and the remainder of the tail hair is left free.

In Scotland (or indeed, wherever Clydesdales are found) a very difficult form of mane plaiting known as a Diamond Roll may be used. This, according to Bobby Woods, chief horseman for James Buchanan & Co., takes well over two hours to complete. It is, in effect, two plaits separated by lengths of mane. It is used widely in harness classes, possibly less so in in-hand classes.

When plaiting, etc., is completed, the horse and its handler are ready to enter the ring in an in-hand class. These classes follow a set pattern in Britain (although, as described in the chapter on Percherons, the procedure is different in Europe), and are possibly a little puzzling to the casual observer not familiar with the finer points of heavy horse judging – the cynical will no doubt say that they are sometimes more than a little puzzling even to those who are!

The horses are led in at the walk, and proceed round the perimeter of the ring in a clockwise direction, while the judge gains his first important impressions. After one or more circuits, the ring stewards, on the judge's instructions, call the exhibitors into line in an approximate order of merit from what has been seen of the horse's side view. (Sometimes, each horse may be asked to walk or trot past the judge individually so that the paces can be seen in profile.) When the class is in line the judge may examine each horse more carefully, then each one will be called out in turn. The exhibitor places his horse carefully in front of the class, making sure it is standing correctly, while the judge makes another, very detailed, inspection. Next, the exhibitor walks his horse away from the judge for some 20 to 30 yds. (18 to 27 m.) turns, and walks him back, and repeats the procedure at the trot. During this, the judge is able to see the horse's action, and make sure that it moves absolutely straight, without either throwing its feet sideways, or crossing them slightly. Finally, the class is probably asked to circle again, before being called in to the final line-up for the award of prizes.

So much for the in-hand classes. But it is in the harness classes and the decorated harness classes that the full glory of heavy-horse decorations are seen. The horses are in full harness, and their owners' imagination can, and usually does, run riot, with brass ornaments, wool and plastic decorations, and bells, combining to make a sparkling and colourful picture. The presence of the full harness offers plenty of sites to which decorations can be attached, and it is these, together with the cleanliness and correct fit, on which the classes are judged. In the decorated harness classes the horse itself is not judged; this gives a chance to exhibitors who do not own show-standard horses.

In Britain the decorations most readily recognised by the general public are probably the horse brasses, as people with little or no 'horsey' connections sometimes collect these attractive and interesting items as a hobby. They are, as the name implies, made of brass, and there are upwards of 2,000 designs, with the numbers still growing. They can be placed almost anywhere on the harness. Most commonly they are found on the face-pieces, the martingale (the martingale in heavy horse harness is a strap that is attached to the collar, runs between the front legs, and is

fastened to the girth underneath the horse, and is more accurately known as a breast strap), the side strap, and the hip strap.

The practice apparently had its origins in the latter half of the 18th century, when brass harness decorations such as buckles and ovals began to appear. It has been suggested that they were lucky charms to ward off evil spirits, but most authorities believe that their real origins lie in the wagoners' desire to copy the more expensively decorated horses belonging to the gentry.

The majority of horse brasses are circular, but there is a variety of other shapes, including crescents, clover leaves, scallops, hearts and shields. The designs, which are stamped or worked on to them, fall into two main types – patterned, on which the design is geometric, and subject brasses, many of which are based on heraldic devices such as dogs, stags, horses, swans and other birds.

Brasses connected with trade, industry and, naturally enough, agriculture, are numerous. Some depict ploughmen and horses; others, doubtless designed for railway horses, show early railway engines; while the timber merchants were represented by crossed saws or trees, and the millers' horses would have been adorned with brasses showing windmills and wheatsheaves.

Individual companies and local councils produced their own designs for 'private brasses' in the hey-days of the carthorse. For example, many of the large breweries such as Shipstones of Nottingham had their own brasses, bearing the name of the company. A number of railway companies also had their own designs, and individual farmers sometimes had brasses bearing the name of their farm.

Two types, the commemorative and the award brasses, appear to have begun at the same time as the decorative brasses. The first commemoratives appeared in the reign of Queen Victoria, around 1870, while other brasses marked the accession of King George V. More recently, the Shire Horse Society's centenary year was commemorated by a special brass.

Award brasses produced on behalf of the Royal Society for the Prevention of Cruelty to Animals, for presentation at the London Cart Horse Parade, appeared around 1886, and following that a number were designed for various local horse shows and parades. In 1947, the London, Midland and Scottish Railway awarded a brass at the parade of their railway horses. The practice has, sadly, rather fallen by the wayside, and the last ones presented may well have been at ploughing matches in southern England.

Horse brasses are by no means the only form of brass ornamentation on harnesses. Hame plates and rosettes are popular items, while fly head terrets are upstanding ornaments, often with moveable metal discs and sometimes with horse-hair plumes, that are worn either in the head strap or on the collar. They also had the useful function of acting as a fly deterrent. Bells, which are popular forms of decoration in some parts of Britain, were also designed for a practical purpose. In Cornwall, for instance, when large teams of horses were used in the china clay workings

Vaux Brewery's unicorn hitch of Percherons in a harness turn-out class at the Durham County Show.

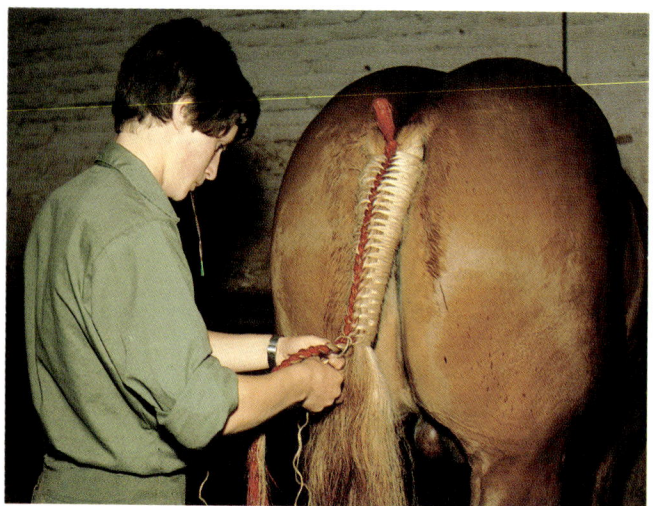

around St Austell, the team leaders used to wear bells in their harness so that when they were making their way home after dark, the teams that followed them could hear which way they had gone.

In Scotland, decoration, and especially at the Royal Highland Show at Edinburgh, harness decoration classes, reach a splendour unsurpassed at any other event in Britain. There are four classes: for best decorated harness, floral; best decorated harness, wool; best groomed horse; and best kept harness.

As in other heavy horse classes the mane and tail are elaborately braided and decorated with ribbons, standards and flowers; but the centre piece of the whole exhibit is the bridge over the saddle, the crown of the collar and the breeching, with additional adornment on the forelock, the bridle, the hames — in fact, anywhere where decorations can reasonably be attached. Decorating harness is almost a cottage industry in Scotland, where exhibitors and their families spend the long winter evenings designing and preparing their display for the coming season. Similarly with woollen classes, which are the older-established of the two, and which employ a marvellous array of pompoms and other intricate items, such as woollen sprays.

Of all the heavy-horse competitions at shows, probably the most popular with the public are the harness turn-outs. They have the dual appeal of beautifully turned-out horses, complete with decorations, and the gleaming, spotless show vehicles, being driven spectacularly round the ring. Be it a single horse, a pair, tandem, unicorn, or a team of four, a turn-out class is a colourful and stirring sight. And the fact that such classes are still held with ever-increasing support is due in large part to the breweries, not just in Britain, but in many other countries, who have done so much to keep the heavy horse in the public eye during the lean years.

In turn-out classes the judge assesses the merits of the horses, the harness, the vehicles and the drivers and grooms. As the turn-outs enter the ring, the judge notes the way the horses are going. Is the team all pulling correctly, are the horses behaving? He looks at the driver to see if he is handling the turn-out well. Is he, for instance, holding the reins correctly? When the turn-outs are called into line, the judge makes a very minute examination of each. First the horses are examined for cleanliness, then the harness — and the competent judge does not take the cleanliness on trust, he looks underneath as well. He will check to see such details as whether all the buckles are of the same metal. The correct fitting of the harness is absolutely vital, as ill-fitting collars, bridles, and so on, can not only cause injury to the horse by rubbing, but can also be positively dangerous to man and horse alike.

The vehicle itself comes in for eagle-eyed inspection for cleanliness, for correct equipment and for safety. A bucket and feed bag are regarded as standard equipment, and if a whip is carried, as it usually is, it should be stored correctly. For vehicles that normally carry lamps, the latter are regarded as essential, they must be not only clean but also in working order, complete with candles. The whole appearance of a turn-out can be marred by careless dress of either driver or groom, and the driver must, of course, be wearing a correct driving apron. The standard of turn-out classes is so high nowadays that judges have an unenviable task, and at the end of the day the points of excellence that separate the top teams are very, very fine.

Ploughing matches are an increasingly popular form of rural competition in Britain, and are also beginning to attract public interest in other countries such as Australia. It augers well for the future of heavy horses on the land that so many men (and a few women) of all ages are skilful enough to compete in these supreme tests of the skill of heavy-horse handling.

In Britain there are two principal types of horse-ploughing classes — high cut and general purpose. The former (sometimes known as crested ploughing) is the more difficult, and when finished looks the most impressive. The furrow in this is about 7 in. (18 cm.) wide and 5 or 6 in. (13 or 15 cm.) deep, and is turned without breaking. It is cut very precisely so that it forms the three sides of a triangle, with the bottom being the longest side, and the two sides being equal and very smooth. It is also called an oat seed furrow, and was used for seed sown by the broadcast method, with the smooth-sided furrow ensuring even placing of the seed.

The general purpose ploughing leaves a flatter furrow, and is midway between high cut and 'broken work' – in the latter the aim is to break the soil completely, rather than have an unbroken side as in the two other types. The ploughs are set with appropriate parts, depending on the type of furrows to be cut.

In competitions each competitor draws lots for the plot he must plough. This measures about 70 or 80 yds. (63 or 72 m.) by 12 yds. (11 m.) plus a 'headland' where the pair of horses and plough has room to turn. The individual plots are marked by a peg, and the ploughman then sets his own white pegs in an absolutely straight line down the plot from the marker peg to act as a guide-line.

Having set his line of pegs and adjusted his plough so that it digs a shallow furrow, the competitor sets off to plough the 'scratch' or 'ripple' furrows — one up and one down — to act as permanent guide-lines. These furrows are close together and are turned towards each other, and this is one of the most difficult and important parts of the competition. The plough is then adjusted for deeper ploughing, and the scratch furrows are re-ploughed. The ploughing then continues, up and down, each side of the original ridge, always turning *right* at the end of each furrow. When the ploughman has completed two full furrows on each side of the ridge, the judges assess his work thus far, and he then continues until half the plot (or less, depending on the rules) is done. This is called the 'gather'.

The remainder of the plot is then ploughed. The ploughman guides his team along the headland to the side of his own plot, and ploughs a furrow away from his own gather and towards the next competitor's plot. From then on, he turns his plough *left*-handed, and continues ploughing around the remaining plot until it is all turned. This, the second half of the plot, is known as the 'split'.

There is, of course, a great deal more to ploughing matches than just piloting the horse up and down. The plough must be adjusted to suit the conditions, the soil on the side of the furrows must remain smooth, and so on. At the end of the day the judges award marks for the straightness of the furrows, for the levelness of the tops of the furrows, and for consistency of width and depth. They also mark the degree to which the ploughman has managed to bury the 'trash' or 'rubbish', such as grass and weeds, and for the 'soil made available', that is, the quantity of soils turned up by the plough from underneath.

At a number of ploughing matches classes for decorated harness are included.

In previous chapters the popularity of pulling contests in America and Canada has been mentioned, and also their introduction into Australia, where they are being featured in a number of draught-horse shows. In concept, pulling contests are simple, being performed either with weights on a kind of sledge known as a stone-boat, to which weights are added, or with a dynamometer, whose resistance can be increased as the contest progresses.

There are usually three sections in American events, determined by the combined weight of the two horses that make up a team. Those weighing under 3,200 lb. (1,450 kg.) are classed as middleweights, while heavyweights over that figure may gross up to 4,700 lb (2,130 kg.). There are a few lightweight competitions for teams between 2,800 and 3,200 lb. (1,269 and 1,450 kg.).

The aim of the contest is to find the team that can pull the greatest load over a distance of $27\frac{1}{2}$ ft. (8.25 m.) that being the distance it has been calculated a team needs to reach its maximum strength, after which its power falls away.

One might expect that the team would be carefully 'put to' the weighted vehicle and the contest would start then; but no – it is much more skilful than that. The horses are not actually attached to the load until the exact moment when they are ready to leap forward and exert maximum 'pull'. To execute each pull requires the finely-timed combined efforts of three to handle the team. There is the driver, who holds the lines and urges the horses on during the actual pull; and there are two 'hookers', who have the tricky task of pulling the horses back to the stoneboat, while at the same time 'geeing them up' to be ready to pull forward instantaneously and together. At that precise moment, the hookers 'hook' the horses to the load, and they leap forward. During the pull, the drivers are not allowed to touch their horses, so there is no question of whipping them on to greater effort; some contests are so strict that the drivers are even forbidden to shout at their teams. The excited spectators, however, make up for the quietness of the drivers by cheering and shouting to urge on their favourites. Each team is allowed three pulls at each weight, and in the end the winner is often the team who can pull the top weight the greatest distance down the measured distance – it may be 20 ft. (6 m.), it may only be 16 ft. (5 m.).

Clearly, for a contest of this kind, training is important, but the massive draught power of breeds such as the Belgians and the Percherons seems to give them an advantage over other breeds.

As described, pulling contests used to be very popular in England, but the practice died out. One or two attempts have been made to revive it in this country, but without success, and if the feelings of one visiting Briton who witnessed an event in Australia are any guide to the general feelings, then they are unlikely to make a comeback. 'I hated it,' he said. 'It tore the horses' guts out.'

So we come to the end of this account of the best known breeds of heavy horses around the world. Almost throughout and in nearly every breed, a constant theme has run. A small band of dedicated owners has refused, in spite of mechanisation, to accept the possibility of extinction for their breed. Against the odds, they devotedly maintained a nucleus of breeding stock and by using them in competition, as working animals, or even for producing meat, they have kept the breeds viable.

Those of us who love and admire the 'gentle giants' – of whichever breed – owe to those breeders an enormous debt of gratitude.

Opposite *Braiding the tail of a Suffolk. Also of interest are the huge muscular quarters so typical of the breed.*

Right *A tinted postcard of 1906 showing Clydesdales wearing Scottish Peaked Collars, popular in Scotland and in North America.*

Bibliography

Baird, Eric. *The Clydesdale Horse*, Batsford, 1982.
Chivers, Keith. *The Shire Horse*, Allen, 1977.
Cockcroft, Barry. *Princes of the Plough*, Dent, 1978.
Ewart Evans, G. *Ask the Fellows Who Cut the Hay*, Faber, 1956.
Ewart Evans, G. *Horse Power & Magic*, Faber, 1979.
Ewart Evans, G. *The Horse in the Furrow*, Faber, 1960.
Glyn, Richard. *The World's Finest Horses & Ponies*, Harrap, 1971.
Harris, Douglas. *The Teams of the Blacksoil Country*, Rohan Rivett, 1977.
Hart, Edward. *Golden Guinea Book of Heavy Horses*, David & Charles, 1976.
Hart, Edward. *Heavy Horses*, Batsford, 1981.
Hartley Edwards, E. (ed.). *Standard Guide to Horse & Pony Breeds*, MacMillan, 1980.
Keegan, Terry. *The Heavy Horse: Its Harness & Decorations*, Pelham Books, 1973.
Suffolk Horse Society. *The Suffolk Horse*, Suffolk Horse Society, 1979.
Verlag, Limpert. *Liebenswerte Riesen*, Papavassiliou, 1980.
Weatherley, Lee. *Great Horses of Britain*, Saiga, 1979.
Whitlock, Ralph. *Gentle Giants*, Lutterworth, 1976.

Acknowledgements

My thanks are due to a number of organisations and individuals around the world, without whose assistance this book could not have been written. These include: Mrs Gloria Frail (Australian Draught Horse Society); Mrs Elwyn Parks (Percheron Horse Breeders Association – Australia); Mr Gavin Cole (British Ardennes Society); Mrs Barbara Meyers (Canadian Belgian Horse Association); Mr Grahame A. West (Shirehorse Society of Australia); The Shire Horse Society (Great Britain); The Clydesdale Horse Society of Great Britain and Ireland; The British Percheron Society; The Suffolk Horse Society; Syndicat Hippique Boulonnais; Avlsforeniggen Den jydske Hest (Denmark); The Agricultural Counsellor and Mr D. P. D. Van Rappard of the Royal Netherlands Embassy, London; Fédération des Syndicats d'Elevage Ardennais; Société Royal Le Cheval de Trait Ardennais (Belgium); La Federation des Sociétiés Hippiques Bretonnes; Percheron Horse Association of America; Mrs Anna Aaby (Denmark); Société Hippique Percheron; Prof Gosta Bengtsson of the College of Veterinary Medicine, Swedish University of Agricultural Sciences, Uppsala; Arbeitsgemeinschaft der Noriaschen Pferdzuchtverbande Osterreichs (Austria); Mr Adam Schmidt of the Hungarian Embassy, London; Mr Frederik Olsen (Denmark); Mrs Anne G. Cunningham (British Embassy, Rome); M. Henry Blanc (Le Chef du Service des Haras, France); Herr Winfried Hackenburg (Germany); Mr Hugh McGregor; Dr Pál Janos (Hungary); Terimpex of Budapest; Mr A. S. Shtorkh (USSR); Mrs B. Klein; M. Meunier (Union Nationale Interprofessionelle du Cheval, Paris); and Mr John Bramley.

My particular thanks and appreciation are due to Mr Robert Owen and Mrs Patricia Pierce of Country Life Books for their help and understanding during the preparation of this book, and to Miss Margaret Saunders, who designed the superb jacket.

Photographs

Colour Animal Photography, London: Sally Anne Thompson 2, 7, 17, 25, 35, 53, 56, 60, 61, 64, 69, 72-73, 77, 84 bottom, 85, 96 bottom; Animal Photography: R. Willbie 43, 65 left, 80, 92-93, 121; Ardea, London: Hans D. Dossenbach 42, 65 right; Ardea: Jean-Paul Ferrero 101, 113, 124; T. Andrew Artha, Hasholme Carr Farm, Holm upon Spalding Moor 96 top, 100, 104-105; Australian Information Service, Canberra 20; Author 76; J. G. Baker, Colchester 112; Gavin Cole, Crook 15; Colour Library International, London 11, 14, 97, 108-109; Y. Le Berre, St. Brieuc 38, 39; Mansell Collection, London 47, 125; Tom Parker, Carnforth 6; Swedish University of Agricultural Sciences, Uppsala 68; Tass, London 84 top, 88-89; ZEFA (U.K.), London 28; ZEFA: K. Jung 117; ZEFA: J. F. Millies 116; ZEFA: E. Weiland 32.

Black and white Animal Photography, London 26; Australian Draught Horse Stud Book Society, Possum Brush, New South Wales 19, 21, 22, 23; Author 78, 95, 99, 102-103, 119 left, 119 right; J. G. Baker, Colchester 111; Gavin Cole, Crook 12, 13, 18, 49, 122-123; Y. de la Fosse-David 37 top; Imperial War Museum, London 74-75, 75 top, 75 bottom; Leslie Lane, Burgess Hill 41, 44-45, 114; Y. Le Berre, St. Brieuc 37 bottom; Machatschek, Paris 71; Mansell Collection, London 10, 34, 40, 67, 91, 93, 98, 107, 120; J. E. McNeil, Burlington, Ontario 31; News Limited, Sydney 9; Orszagos Lotenyesztesi Felugyeloseg 54, 55; PAF International, London 57, 58-59; Pferdestammbuch Scheswig-Holstein, Hamburg 90; Royal Netherlands Embassy, London 50; Jos. Schlitz Brewing Company, Milwaukee, Wisconsin 27; Sport & General Press Agency, London 79, 115; VAAP, Moskva 83, 86, 87; M. Schnitzhofer 63; John Topham Picture Library, London 8; Westfälisches Pferdestammbuch, Münster 81; ZEFA, London: F. Walther 51.

Index

N.B.: Page numbers in *italic* refer to illustrations

Aberdeen District Council Parks Department *45*, 48
Aldrup 59
Aldrup-Munkedal 58 *et seq.*
American Shire Horse Society 103 *et seq.*
Arabs 25, 27, 33, 36, 56, 70, 72
Ardennes 12-18, *12-15*, *17*, *18*, 39, 50, 52, 54, 80, 81, 82, 86, 94; Annual Breed Show, Vittel 12, 17; Auxois type 15; Belgian Ardennes 17-18; Belgian Ardennes show successes; Belgian Heavy Draught blood 15; British Ardennes 16; 'Classic' 15; colours 15; description of French Ardennes 16; evolution on Franco-Belgian borders 12; French Ardennes 15-17; French Stud Book 16; introduction of Oriental blood 15; meat production 15; Northern Ardennes 15; principal breeding areas in France 15; Swedish Ardennes 60, 88; Trait du Nord 15-16; types of Ardennes 15; use in other breeds 18; use as war horses 15; use by Marshal Turenne 12; use in Hungary 52, 54.
Australia History of Heavy breeds 19-23
Australian Draught Horse 7, 19-24, *19-23*, 71, 111; bore drain delving 23; breed standard 24; foundation of Stud Book and Breed Society 24; other breeds 19, *118*; origins 19; 'Teams of the Blacksoil Plains' 19; tank construction 19.
Australian Percheron Breeders' Association 71

Baird, Eric, *The Clydesdale Horse* 44, 48
Baptiste de la Croyette 27
Baron of Buchlyvie
Baron's Pride 44
Belgian Heavy Draught 15, 16, 25-31, *25-8*, *31*, *32*, 50, 54, 63, 65, 66, 80, 86; Albion d'Hor 29; Arab blood 25, 27; Breed Society 29; Brilliant, son of Orange I 29; Colosses de la Mehaigne 27; description 25; Forty Horse Hitch 30; Greys of Hainaut 27; Gros de la Dendre type 27; in Denmark 29; in USA & Canada 29-31; infusions of other blood 27; infusions of Shire blood 27; Jupiter 29; Oreins, August 29 *et seq.*; Orange I 27-29.
Biddell, Hermann 108 *et seq.*
Bird, Roy 102
Blaze, Early English Draught Horse in Scotland 43
Boulonnais 33-39, *34-5*, 56, 80, 90, 93; Arab influence on, 33; depletion during World Wars 34; description 33; Gros Boulonnias 34; Mecklenberg blood 34; Petit Boulonnais 34-35; principal breeding areas 33; 17th-century types 34; use in development of other breeds 35; uses today 34-5.
Bramley, John 110
Breton 35, 36-9, *37-9*, 56, 90; Arab influence 36; description 36; effect of French Revolution 36, 38; meat production 39; Norfolk Trotter blood 36, 39; other foreign blood 36, 39; Petit Breton 36; post-First-World-War types 39; Postier Breton 36; present numbers 39; principal breeding areas 36; Roussin type 36; Sommier type 36; Stud Book 39; Trait Breton type 36.
British Percheron Breed Society 77-8
Buchanan, James & Co., 47-8

Caesar, Julius 12, 33
Carling O'Keefe Breweries 31

Carlsberg Breweries 31, 66
Chester, Clydesdale gelding 47-8
Chivers, Keith, *The Shire Horse* 78, 88, 100
Clark, Roger 10, 110
Clyde (Glancer 153) 43
Clydesdale 9, 16, 19, 21, 23, 24, 40-49, *41-5*, *47*, *49*, 63, 65, 66, 76, 80, 83, 94, 100, 101, 102, 104, *115*, 118, 119, 121, *121*, *125*; 'Clyde' versus Shire 41; description 40-42; Drew, Lawrence 47 *et seq.*; famous stallions 44; Hamilton, Duke of 43; in Australia 23, 49; in New Zealand 49; in USA & Canada 40, 48; introduction of Flemish blood 43; origins 42; Paterson of Lochlyoch 43; present uses 47, 48; Riddell, David 46 *et seq.*; Select Clydesdale Horse Society 46, 47; Stud Book and Society 46; travelling stallions 43.
Clydesdale Breeders' Association (USA) 48
Cole, Gavin S. 16
Competition 118-25; grooming 118-19; judging of show classes 119; harness decoration classes 121; ploughing matches 124-25; preparation for showing 118; pulling contests 125.
Constantin Period (Jutland) 58
Crisp's Horse of Ufford 108-9
Cullum, Rev. Sir John 107-8
Cumberland 48

Darnley 222 48
Diluvial horse. See Forest/Diluvial horse
Drew, Lawrence 46 *et seq.*
Dunmor, Earl of 46
Dunure Footprint 44, 45
Dutch Heavy Draught Horse 16, 25, 50-51, *50-51*; annual inspection 50-51; description 50; origins 50; Stud Book 50; uses 50-51.
Dykes, Thomas 43

Ewart Evans, G. 106
Elizabeth I, Queen 95
Elizabeth II, Queen 94, *102*
Ellesmere, Earl of 100
English Cart Horse Society 101 *et seq.*

Field Marshal 102
Flemish/Flanders horse 9, *10*, 25, 33, 43, 95
Forest/Diluvial horse 9, 25
Frail, Mr Mal 24

George V, King 102
Gilbey, Sir Walter 100
'Glancer 335' 43
Grand National 47
Great War Horses 94-5
Gros de Wynhuyze 27

Hales Argo & Hales Chiron 71
Harness 114-15, *115*, 124, 125
Harris, Douglas 19 *et seq.*, 22, 23

Heavy Horse Driving Magazine 16
Holland, Albert 102
Hollesley Bay Borstal 110-11
Hoorebeke, Dr A. G. 29
Horse Brasses 123-4
Horserace Betting Levy Board 102
Hungarian Breeds 52-5
Hungarian Heavy Draught 54-5, *53-5*; care of foals; description 54; origins 54; performance tests 55; uses 55

Italian Heavy Draught or Agricultural Heavy 56, *56*

Jean le Blanc 70
Jorgenson, Stan 49
Jutland 7, 29, 57-60, *57-61*, 80, 90, 111; decline 58; description 57; development 57-8; influence of Suffolks 57, 60; influence on Schleswig-Holsteins 60; standards 58-9; Stud Book 57, 58; uses 60

Kamiloroi Stud 72
Kay, Mr David 102

Lampits mare 43
Lincolnshire type of heavy horse 99
Lithuanian Heavy Harness *83*, 88, *88-9*; description 88; origins 88; performance 88; recognition 88; Stud Book 88; studs 88.

Manes, plaiting of 119-20; Full rig 119-20; Half rig 119-20; Diamond Roll 121.
Murakozi 52-5, *53-5*
McGregor, Hugh 49

Newstead Percheron Stud 71, 72
Norfolk Trotters 36, 39, 52, 56
Noriker *2*, 52, 62-8, *63-5*; colours 62; breeding programmes 62-3, 65; decline in numbers 63; description 62; early studs 62; government control 65; history 62; influence of monasteries 62; in Hungary 52; Pinzgau Noriker 65; principal blood lines 65; regional variations 63; Stud Book 62; uses 62-3.
Northern or Coldblood Horses 9
North Swedish 60, 66-9, *67-9*; description 66; development 66; draught tests 66-7; influence of Norwegian Dole 66; official recognition 66; role of veterinary profession 66; selection of colts 66; survey of horses 67-8; uses in lumbering 67-8; Wangen stallion rearing institution 66; working in forests 67 *et seq.*
Norwegian Dole (Gudbransdal) 66

Olsen, Frederick 29
Oppenheim (Jutland) 57 *et seq.*
Oreins, Auguste 29 *et seq.*

Packington Blind Horse 98
Park, Mr & Mrs R. G. 72
Pedersen, Nils 58
Percheron Horse Society of America 73
Percheron 19, 21, 24, 33, 39, 52, 70-79, *71-3, 76-9*, 80, 86, 102, 104, *118*, 120, *122-3*; annual show in France 79; Arab influence 70; British Percheron Society 78; description 70, 78; effect of French Revolution 70; Grand Taille 71; history 70; importance in First World War 76; in Australia 71; in Falkland Islands 71; in Hungarian breeds 52, 54; in USA 71-3; introduction to Britain 76-7; Petit Taille (Postier) 71; present types 70; principal breedings areas in France 70; Stud Book 71; sub-races 70-71; uses 70.
Pinkafoi 52
Ploughing matches 124-5

Prince of Wales (Edward VII) 46
Prince of Wales 673 44, 46
Prince William 101
Pulling contests 72-3, 106, 125

Rhenish-German 80-81, *80-81*; breeding programme 80; decline in numbers 80; description 81; influence on Hessen Heavy Horse 81; influence on Westphalian horse 81; variation in types 80-81; Wickrath Stud 81.
Roughlands Telstar 49
Rowntree, David 48
Royal Association of The Netherlands Heavy Horse 50
Royal Society of Ardennais Heavy Horse 17, 18
Russian Breeds 82-9, *83-9*
Russian Heavy Draught 82, *84-5*; crosses with Soviet Heavy Draught 82; description 82; fertility 82; official recognition 82; performance records 82; studs 82; uses 82.

Schleswig-Holstein 35, 90-93, *90-93*; Breed Society 93; decline in numbers 90; description 90; history 90; influence of other breeds 90; introduction of Jutlands 93; Society of Schleswig Breeders 90.
Schwarz Walker Chestnut 65
Shirehorse Society of Australia 104
Shires 6, 9, *10*, 16, 19, 21, 24, 27, 33, 40, 41, 43, 46, 57, 73, 76, 78, 80, 83, 94-104, *95-105*, *114*, 118, 119, *119*, 121; 'Blacks' in the Fens 98; Breed Society 101, 102; cart-horses 99; centenary show 94; decline after Second World War 102; description 94; discussion of development 94-5; draining of Fens 98; export trade 103 *et seq.*; greasy legs 102; in America 103 *et seq.*; in Australia 104; in development of Belgian Heavy 27; in New Zealand 104; Stallion Hiring Society 100; Stallion Premium scheme 102; Stud Book 101; uses 100.
Sir Everard 44
Skjalden (Jutland) 59
South German Heavy 65
Soviet Heavy Draught 86-9, *86*; blood lines 86; description 86; development 86; female line 86; performance tests 88; principal breeding areas 86.
Sparrow, Dick, & Forty Horse Hitch 30
Standard Cyclopedia of Modern Agriculture 41
Suffolk 10, 16, 19, 21, 24, 40, 57, 60, 80, 86, 94, 106-11, *107-9*, *111-13*, 119, 120; Breaking-in centre 110; Breed Society 110; breeding scheme of 1897 110; colours 106; description 106; 'drawing matches' 106; exports 111; importance of Crisp's Horse of Ufford 108; oldest established British breed 106; origins in East Anglia 108; performance tests in 18th century 106; Premium scheme 110; side bone 110; Stud Book 109-10; typical working day 110; uses 110.
Swedish Ardennes 18, 60, 88

Tails, Braiding of 120-21; Percherons 120; Shires 120; Suffolks 120.
Turenne, Viscount 12

Valdemar Period (Jutland) 58
Victoria, Queen 46
Vladimir Heavy Draught 82-6, *85, 87*; description 82, 86; evolution 83; influence of Clydesdales 83; performance records 83; uses 83.

West, Grahame 104
Westphalian Heavy Draught. See The Rhenish-German Heavy
William the Conqueror 101
Winther, Anders 59
Woods, Bobby (of James Buchanan & Sons) 47-8, 121